Earth Talk

Earth Talk

Independent Voices on the Environment

Tom Artin

Grossman Publishers   New York   1973

for Mrs. Scruggs,
who liked what I wrote

Preface

I wouldn't have written this book had the idea for it not occured to Dick Kaplan, and had he not in turn interested Dick Grossman in printing it. So to both of them go my first thanks. A load of thanks also to Tom Stewart, who edited the book with understanding, appreciation, and a hawk-sharp eye for nonsense, bad taste, and errors of fact—the sort of editor writers usually have to wish they had. Special thanks to Loffe Norrman and Annika Sjöblom, my friends in Stockholm who fed and housed me in their elf cottage the last week and a half of my stay there. And finally, more than thanks to Phee, who stayed home and slept on my side of the bed, who read and listened to sections of the manuscript that has been an excuse for so many things for a year, and who is going through with the wedding anyway.

Contents

Earth Talk

I

Getting There

Stockholm was a fine place, quite perfect for this gathering of politicians and scientists and ordinary citizens, who came from all over the globe to talk about environment. "Queen of Lake Mälar," Stockholm is called, situated on either side of the channel through which the sweet waters of the island-studded lake flow eastward into the mild Saltsjö ("Saltsea") of the outer archipelago and beyond into the Baltic. The lake flows beautifully under bridges among the islands of the city. Spires and belfries and the famous tower of the town hall rise above buildings of Nordic, slightly austere baroque. On the central island, the tightly packed, narrow streets of Gamla Stan ("Old Town") recall its medieval origins; on a smaller island connected to it by bridges the Victorian Old Parliament Building, headquarters for the United Nations Conference on the Human Environment, sits like a marble lion. A few boats move through the water; others are tied along the quays, large Baltic ferries, cargo ships, smaller sightseeing boats. In the nearly un-broken sunshine of this June—the weather seems to con-spire with the Swedish authorities—the water glistens, and the city has, at odd moments, the shine of glass.

At moments—for Stockholm is not a magical city. It is a very real one. Real people live and work here, in real houses, at real jobs. It is sometimes called "the Venice of the North," but this amounts to false advertising; Stockholm is not a museum or a monument to the past. You are jostled in the buses and subways by real commuters, getting in and out of the city as they do in Philadelphia or Wichita. A millenium ago, centuries before the founding of Stockholm, a thriving center of Viking trade existed to the west on Björkö ("Birch-Isle"), further into Lake Mälar, where it was protected even more than Stockholm is by the labyrinth of rocky, wooded islands between which merchant ships had to pass observed to reach it—thirty miles through the outer archipelago, then eighteen miles more of tortuous navigation within the lake. Björkö (or Birka, as it was called by foreign writers of the time) was the vital center of a Swedish trade that reached to England and Frisia in the west and to the Volga in the east, and certainly it was realism, not paranoia, that led the hardy Vikings to situate their capital in such security. By the same token, however, the security of Mälar's islands was extended by law to all who came there to trade in peace. "The Frisian, Dane, German, Englishman, Finn, Swede, Balt, Greek or Arab (if he ever showed up) was offered safety and fair play; the townsmen and local traders could look to the peaceful pursuit of riches; and the king who safeguarded these processes enjoyed esteem, privilege, and profit."[1] For all their legendary ferocity, the Vikings apparently knew when peace was good for business.

Probably a break that occurred in the eastern trade in the second half of the tenth century accounted for Björkö's rather sudden demise. In the eleventh century, Sigtuna, situated on a northern arm of the lake, took over as the center of Swedish trade. In the middle of the thirteenth century, with the decline of piracy in the Baltic, the Swedish regent Birger Jarl, who is credited with laying the foundations of Sweden's overseas empire through his military expedition into Finland, established Stockholm—further east, appropriately, toward the open sea—as the chief market for trade with Lübeck, as well as with the other commercial towns that had sprung up on the shores of the Baltic. Yet there

[1] Gwyn Jones, *A History of the Vikings* (London: Oxford University Press, 1968), p. 173.

remained cause to be wary. If Stockholm's situation reflected the relatively more secure commerce of the thirteenth century, it was nevertheless a strategic spot, commanding the entrance to the lake. The city was built as a fortress, from which it got its name, Stock-holm ("Log-Island"), testifying still to that defensive, not to say pugnacious, and in any event realistic stance of its commercial foundations.

Today, that defensiveness is barely visible. Stockholm, unlike Philadelphia or Wichita, is a truly civilized city, a city of culture, a city in which it is possible to walk at night without the fear of violence. Vikings no longer lurk there —they are only sold as fuzzy souvenirs with tiny bellies. Stockholm was all blue-eyed smiles and helpfulness for the big conference—the United Nations Conference on the Human Environment, which Sweden herself four years earlier had suggested the need for, and which therefore appropriately (and at Sweden's express and gracious invitation) was to be held in her capital city from the fifth to the sixteenth of June, 1972. The Swedes were eager to please everyone—Frisian, Dane, German, Greek, Arab, even Chinese or Russian (if he ever showed up). In a world torn apart by war, disease, injustice, and famine, Sweden was a harbor of safety, an example to the rest of the world of peace and order and enlightened social policy—a place to begin putting the world right.

No Vikings. Still, there were police—thousands of them, called in from all over the country and specially trained for months ahead of time to keep the peace in Stockholm. The cops were everywhere, on foot, on horseback, on motorcycles, in cars, in phalanxes, in twos and threes, by the troop, by the busload. On horses they looked grimly medieval in their shiny new riot helmets, visors up. At the drop of a hat, or a questionable remark (let alone a paving stone) the fatigue-clad canine corps would let their dogs, growling and straining fiercely at their leashes, out of the waiting vans. Busloads of cops showed up at every demonstration, and every occasion that might turn into a demonstration. The night I attended the Royal Opera's special United Nations Conference production of Verdi's "A Masked Ball," for instance, the opera house was ringed by police buses, while groups of three or four policemen milled out front in the square—although the house was only half full, and the streets were virtually deserted. The cops looked bored, but the authorities weren't taking any chances. Verdi's opera, which deals with the assassination of the Swedish king Gustaf II, was orginally banned by the censor of Rome, who found a regicide far too inflammatory to present on stage. Maybe the Swedish police were swayed by the censor's logic.

Swedish officialdom had expected thousands of militant youths—"eco-freaks" and peaceniks—to converge on Stockholm and disrupt the city and the conference as a focus for protest. I couldn't help feeling that the cops were increasingly disappointed as the days and then the weeks went by without much real action. They were ready for it—just as Sweden, which boasts 150 years of noninvolvement in war, is nevertheless ready to protect itself against invasion or attack with an elaborate and costly defense network that includes universal military training, strategic underground factories, camouflaged ships, and artillery hidden in rocks and hillsides around its borders. They were ready for action; it just never came.

On the other hand, although the Swedish police apparently had dreams of the likes of the Democratic Party's 1968 convention, they behaved differently from the Chicago police in the crunch. At an all-night vigil to protest the French atomic test at Mururoa Atoll (conducted only shortly after the United Nations Conference on the Human Environment [UNCHE] resolved to condemn all nuclear-weapons testing, especially that carried out in the atmosphere, and called "upon those States intending to carry out nuclear weapons tests to abandon their plans to carry out such tests since they may lead to further contamination of the environment") someone leaned against the already cracked glass door of a store, and broke it. In a flash, a cluster of cops surrounded the hapless demonstrator, and were leading him away, as a hundred or so more appeared from where they had been watching and surrounded the sixty or seventy peaceful demonstrators who were sitting in the square, singing and acting out an atomic explosion in mime. One of the cops took a bullhorn and announced dramatically (he'd trained for this for six months), "You must go away, in ones and twos, in different directions." It wasn't a particularly confrontational crowd, but no one moved. Someone from the Canadian Green Peace movement, which had called the demonstration, went over to the bullhorner and patiently explained that the glass door had been broken by accident, that this was a peaceful protest, that the people had come to try to stop an explosion that would do harm to other people. Deep down, obviously, the police weren't confrontational either, because they changed their minds. As one of the conference daily news sheets put it, "the 100 police went away in ones and twos, in different directions. Quietly, the singing continued. The vigil went on."

The overanxious, oversupplied police were clearly someone's good intention, not the instrument of counter-revolutionary violence. Sweden's best foot was forward, and it just didn't want the shoe scuffed, especially not by a bunch of hippies and anarchists. To make sure we got all the facts about that best foot, the city of Stockholm gave each of the 1200 (some said 1600) accredited correspondents a gift of a snappy black vinyl portfolio, embossed with the emblem of the conference and the legend "Stockholm 1972." It was a weighty gift, bulging with literature promoting the virtues of Sweden in general and Stockholm in particular. The major theme, of course, was Sweden's leadership in environmental protection. A series of five slick paper brochures illustrated Stockholm's dynamic approaches to the five major problem areas of modern urbanization, housing, water, solid-waste disposal, energy production, and transportation. Other pamphlets told how Swedish industry is doing all it can to help clean up the environment, how the government is instituting bold programs of control and improvement, and how Sweden has licked just about all the problems a country can have. The vinyl package also had some goodies—a free pass for all the city's public transportation, a free pass to all museums and parks, an invitation to what turned out to be a lavish reception given by the city in the garden of the town hall for delegates and correspondents, a first-day-of-issue cover of the conference commemorative stamps, and a thoroughly superfluous vinyl secretary with a pad of lined paper to take notes on and a ballpoint pen to take them with.

The irony of the vinyl gift was hard to ignore. To begin with, plastics manufacture is highly polluting, primarily because it requires so much heat. There was a great deal of talk in all the forums at Stockholm of the need to replace synthetic with natural materials wherever possible. Second, vinyl is one of the worst plastics. Barry Commoner reports in *The Closing Circle* that vinyl exudes an ooze over extended periods of time which is probably poisonous.[2] But Sweden is quite gone on plastics. The plastic things you buy in the stores come wrapped in plastic, and then get put in plastic bags to take them home in. The shelves of stores are laden with brightly colored, shiny, rakishly designed, seductive plastic things—plastic cups, plastic plates, plastic forks and spoons, plastic jugs, plastic coats, plastic scissors, plastic tables and chairs, plastic boats. I used my plastic portfolio for two days because I have a hard time turning down anything that's free. But I got to feeling creepy handling it without gloves, so I threw it away along with the matching plastic secretary and ballpoint pen and the several pounds of public relations, which must have taken a small acre or two of forest to print.

One consultant to the United Nations Conference Secretariat, an economist from Senegal who had taken part in the preconference meeting at Founex, Switzerland, to consider problems of environment and development, expressed concern not only that Sweden's hosting of the conference was essentially a public relations venture, but even that interest in environmental problems in countries such as

[2] Barry Commoner, *The Closing Circle* (New York: Alfred A. Knopf, 1971), pp. 227–231.

Sweden is motivated largely by investment in the new pollution-control technology. An informed Swedish journalist to whom I repeated this cynical allegation denied that it was worthwhile for Sweden to compete in this field with the United States and Japan, but offered another economic motive for the conference. Sweden's relatively strong anti-pollution legislation makes it difficult for her industries to compete on the international market with industries in countries that have less strict controls or none at all. Thus, it is a matter of self-interest to persuade other countries—particuularly the countries with whom she trades—to establish equally stringent (i.e., expensive) regulations.

The ironies of the conference setting abounded. Saab and Volvo, for instance, provided the conference with its official cars, marked with the conference seal, driven by uniformed lady chauffeurs. They zipped around Stockholm, which is already plagued with an automobile density equal to that of Los Angeles, their exhaust adding to the city's surprisingly acrid air, at roughly the same time that Volvo was joining the four major American automobile manufacturers in appealing the U.S. Environmental Protection Administration's 1975 deadline for compliance with the new, stricter exhaust-emission standards. A pamphlet put out by one of the Swedish counterconference groups was entitled "Don't Trust the U.N. Conference" and called it baldly, "publicity for Sweden, Ltd." "The national committee views the conference as a splendid opportunity to promote Sweden," it said. "Excursions to purifying plants and the like are planned. Saab and Volvo are placing cars at the disposal of each delegation! . . . It will be a very expensive affair. The flag decorations alone will cost 10,000 dollars." Indeed, one of the brochures in the official vinyl portfolio included a schedule of "study tours" and "seminars" arranged by the Federation of Swedish Industries for delegates and correspondents to "See for yourself how industry in Sweden is working to improve the environment. Get the information you want first-hand from experts who deal with the issues. . . . See 'how the Swedes do it.' "

There were other Swedes who were less than enchanted

by the official sweetness and light of government and industry. All over town, people were wearing a white button with
a green elm tree on it, with the legend "grönare stad"
("greener city") underneath. The elm commemorates the
people's saving of a grove of elms in the city's central park,
Kungsträdgård, two years ago. The trees had been slated
for removal because their root systems threatened to inter-
fere with a proposed subway station and underground drug-
store. A local movement concerned with the quality of life
in greater Stockholm called Alternativ Stad ("Alternative
City") organized citizens to guard the trees with their
bodies day and night for over a week, until finally the men
with the chain saws went away, and the engineers and city
planners behind them gave up sending them back. The elms
have become the symbol in Stockholm of public resistance
to the plans of the technocrats. Alternative City's newspaper is called *Almbladet* (*The Elm Leaf*). An ongoing
project, begun two summers ago, is to gather up discarded
bicycles, repair and repaint them, and loan them to tourists
for pollution-free sightseeing. During the weeks of UNCHE
this "alternative sightseeing" was promoted by Alternative
City as a means of countering both official Swedish propaganda to conference guests and the preconference U.N.
document on the environmental aspects of urbanization.
"You have an unique chance," their flier announced, "to
ride on bicycle through the more *and* less beautiful parts
of Stockholm, to see the problems of Stockholm and city
planning as we—and not the U.N. Conference—look at
them."

This campaign was less an attack on UNCHE than a
part of the group's organized resistance to the official
regional master plan for greater Stockholm. By far the
bulkiest piece of propaganda in the vinyl package was a
large, chicly oblong, softbound book, lavishly illustrated on
flashy double-page foldouts with photographs, maps, graphs,
and architect's renderings, describing this regional plan in six
languages. *Stockholm—Urban Environment* the book is
called, and it reports in glowing terms the development of
several satellite communities in the city's suburbs, as well as

the redevelopment of the city's center. It is a pitch couched in the trendy jargon of the planners. The authors write, for example, that in planning the new Tensta district, "the object . . . was to create a partially new type of satellite environment: a residential environment that would combine the intensity, concentration and right-angled regularity of the urban ambience with verdure, space and peace." An aerial photograph on the next page, however, reveals Tensta to be an unusually dreary and tightly packed cluster of high- and low-rise rectangular solids, whose planning was a simple matter of engineering efficiency and had nothing whatever to do with the fancy-sounding urban aesthetic of "intensity, concentration and right-angled regularity." Along with this seductive gobbledygook goes a pretense of objectivity. The authors try to undercut movements such as Alternative City (which they identify by name) by seemingly fair-mindedly taking their criticism into account, then snidely dismissing it. "What do these people seem to want?" they ask. "Argument runs along two lines: save more of the existing buildings and banish private cars from the city center. Even for the new parts of the suburban belt, they demand that private cars be pushed out of the picture, while the bus-and-rail system should be improved and—say many—made free of charge. They object to being the 'victims' of planning and curse when playgrounds and day nurseries are not ready when they move into the newly built dwellings. How common are such opinions? Probably it is only a minority that expresses its discontent, sometimes very noisily—but also cleverly."

This summary of organized criticism of official planning simply ignores the major arguments of Alternative City, which charges first of all that planning in Sweden is based on a policy of accommodation to the industrial interests that the government bureaucracy chiefly serves. Both bureaucratic and industrial interests are served in turn by "rationalization" of production and distribution, which entails concentration of population (the labor force and the consuming public) into metropolitan centers. The regional plan for Stockholm, for instance, is predicated on the projection that the city's population will double within thirty years. But this becomes a self-fulfilling, not a disinterested prophecy, since the plan calls for massive government investment in the metropolitan area, while investment is to be withdrawn from smaller towns and rural areas, which are judged not to have a viable economic future. Essential social services are discontinued in the countryside; small businesses and farms are forced out of competition by the giant corporations with whom the government cooperates; jobs follow the concentration of industry to the city. Alternative City charges that this kind of planning, which ensures the fulfillment of the projections on which it is based, is not only circular and thus faulty, but amounts to an official policy of human manipulation for the sake of profit and bureaucratic efficiency. The regional and national plans are systematically depopulating the countryside by forcing people into a few metropolitan centers. This concentration in turn simply feeds the disastrous environmental problems by which the cities of the world are already beset, and Stockholm, for all its rational planning, is not immune to them.

Now Sweden is a small, prosperous country with an enlightened government. It faces none of the really apocalyptic horrors that threaten billions of others over the globe —at least not immediately. The struggle in Sweden over planning for its three or four major urban centers is, from a global viewpoint, only a local issue. Yet the Alternative City movement, in the context of the United Nations Conference on the Human Environment, puts in focus the profound gulf fixed between the self-justifying power and technology of industry and government, on the one hand, and real human needs and cultural values, on the other. The Alternative City people have no illusions that they can appeal for aid and comfort to the U.N., an organization of and for the national governments of member states—bureaucracies tied, like Sweden's, to the interests of industry and commerce. Increasing urbanization, "rationalization" through concentration, is in the interest of industry and commerce, as well as of government bureaucracy whether in Sweden or the United States or the Soviet Union; the U.N., itself a bureaucracy, is thus concerned only with bringing the process under control, not with reversing it.

A dozen miles outside Stockholm on one of the large islands of the archipelago, the week before the start of UNCHE, an independent conference was convened to discuss the environment. It was sponsored by Dai Dong, a transnational peace effort of the International Fellowship of Reconciliation formed in response to the growing sense that the peace movement had become hamstrung by its exclusive concern with U.S. military disengagement from Indochina, and that the movement needed to go beyond the old pattern of reacting to crises only after they had occurred. While other organizations of public concern focus on some particular problem—war, say, or pollution, or overpopulation, or justice in the third world—Dai Dong focuses on the interrelation of all these problems. Thus, Dai Dong is not specifically an environmentalist organization, or specifically a peace organization, but is based on an analysis that sees the world as a single functioning system in which nothing is independent. War and pollution are only two of the legs of what is in reality a many-legged beast; famine and disease and racism and overpopulation and imperialist exploitation are also legs, and the beast is itself, in turn, an organic part of its historical environment. When the environmental crisis came into the spotlight during "Earth Week" in April, 1970, many people in the peace movement felt that concern for ecology would drain public attention away from the war in Indochina, just as the war issue itself had seemed to threaten to obscure the struggle for civil rights and black liberation in the mid-sixties. Some even saw it as a conspiracy to that end, a planned attempt to "co-opt" the antiwar movement. Dai Dong is convinced that racism and war and environmental deterioration are interrelated aspects of the same system—a system, moreover, not confined within the borders of one country, or peculiar to one socioeconomic ideology, but one that encompasses the globe and all its people. We are all sitting together in one leaky boat, it says, and we must grow beyond the differences that now appear to divide us if we hope to keep the boat from sinking.

The name "Dai Dong" (the whole phrase is "Dai Dong Thé Gioi" which means literally "world of the great togetherness") comes from a pre-Confucian vision of a world in which all people are united as one family. The purpose of the movement is to begin to build that sense of world community by dramatizing through a variety of actions the interrelatedness of our global problems, and the practical (not to say moral) necessity of coming together to solve them. Its aims are hopelessly ambitious of course. But, say the people at Dai Dong, human beings have determined for the earth such a terrible future that only what now seems a desperate and impossible leap gives us any chance at all of altering the probabilities of disaster.

Dai Dong's first project was to bring together six biologists from five countries at Menton, France, in May of 1970, to articulate the nature and suggest the interrelatedness of the problems that in concert confront the globe with its present apocalyptic future. Man has arrived at a point in his evolutionary journey at which he can effectively and in a variety of ways annihilate his own species, possibly all life on the planet. Global politics have been such, however, that he has gone down this path virtually in the dark. Scientific and technological advances, industrial development, commercial and national expansion have all been pursued for relatively short-term benefits, in ignorance of the intricate ways in which all human activity impinges on the present and future environment. Since man has had no sense of global or species loyalty, but has, on the contrary, been set against his neighbor in continual competition, he has acted chiefly out of a narrowly conceived self-interest—or rather, a concept of self-interest that has become narrow in the light of the now inescapable connections between self-interest and the interests of all. For most of human existence, survival has depended on a sense of separateness and an ability to compete aggressively for sustenance and shelter. Suddenly the opposite is true; man's survival now depends on his capacity to transcend his separateness, both from other men, and from the environment itself, which has often seemed alien and hostile, a threat to be mastered.

The biologists at Menton, and the more than three thousand others around the world who have since joined in signing the document they prepared, addressed their "Message" to "our 3.5 Billion Neighbors on Planet Earth." "Widely separated though we are geographically," the Menton Statement begins, "with very different cultures, languages, attitudes, political and religious loyalties, we are united in our time by an unprecedented common danger." The biologists spoke of four broad problem areas—environmental deterioration, depletion of natural resources, population and hunger, and war—and called for the developed nations to embark on a crash program of research, comparable in scope and urgency to the Manhattan Project or the race to the moon, to discover and delineate the precise nature and dimensions of the problems that beset the world and to formulate long-range solutions to them. "We really do not know the full dimensions of either our problems or their solutions," they admitted. "We do know that Earth and all of its inhabitants are in trouble and that our problems will multiply if we do not attend to them." As immediate, short-term measures, the statement called for a moratorium on technological innovations whose environmental effects are not entirely known, strict application of existing antipollution and conservation technologies, programs to curb population growth, and the abolition of war. "Earth, which has seemed so large, must now be seen in its smallness. We live in a closed system, absolutely dependent on Earth and on each other for our lives and those of succeeding generations. The many things that divide us are therefore of infinitely less importance than the interdependence and danger that unite us." The Menton meeting was a small flashlight in the darkness through which we have been stumbling. The message is that we had better see where we are putting our foot before we take the next step.

In May of 1971, the six Menton biologists (among them Conrad Istock and Donald Chant, who were also participants in Dai Dong's Independent Conference in Sweden) together with Alfred Hassler, executive director of Dai Dong, presented the statement, by then signed by more than two thousand biologists, to U Thant, secretary-general of the United Nations, and Maurice Strong, secretary-general of the upcoming United Nations Conference on the Human Environment. Both officials were encouraging. "I believe that mankind is at last aware of the fact that there is a delicate equilibrium of physical and biological phenomena on and around the earth which cannot be thoughtlessly disturbed as we race along the road of technological development," U Thant declared in accepting the statement. "This global concern in the face of a grave common danger, which carries the seeds of extinction for the human species, may well prove to be the elusive force which can bind men together. The battle for human survival can only be won by all nations joining together in a concerted drive to preserve life on this planet." UNESCO's *Courier*, a United Nations Educational, Scientific and Cultural Organization magazine published in twelve languages, with a worldwide circulation of 500,000, printed the Menton Statement as its cover story in the July, 1971, issue.

In spite of their favorable reception, the biologists took the opportunity of their meeting with Strong to express their concern that scientists had not been properly consulted in the preparations for UNCHE. Moreover, since most governments were making political and diplomatic appointments of delegates to the conference, biologists and other scientists would function only in consultative, not decision-making roles at the conference itself. Strong was sympathetic to their criticism, and promised to do whatever he could to see that proper scientific input was included in conference preparations, but he explained that the structure of the United Nations, and specifically of UNCHE, was such that he could make no guarantees. Ultimately, it is the national governments who make up the United Nations that have that power, not the secretariat.

However it was, within a few weeks of the meeting, Maurice Strong appointed René Dubos, microbiologist and experimental pathologist, to chair a group of experts that was to prepare a background report for the delegates to UNCHE and the general public. Strong's letter of appointment explained that the report would "represent the knowledge and opinion of the world's leading experts and thinkers about the relationships between man and his natural habitat at a time when human activity is having profound effects upon the environment." Although the report was commissioned by the UNCHE Secretariat, it was funded independently by Columbia University, the International Bank for Reconstruction and Development (World Bank), and the Ford Foundation. Strong touched on the problematic relations between independent scientific opinion and international politics in his preface to the report, later published as *Only One Earth*. "This report has been considered an integral part of preparations for the United Nations Conference. At the same time it is the work of individuals, serving in their personal capacities without restraints imposed upon officials of governments and international agencies. Thus the report is not an official United Nations document but a report *to* the United Nations Conference Secretariat from an independent expert group. The only restraint on those who prepared the report was a request that they not prejudge the work of governments at the United Nations Conference by proposing specific international agreements or actions—its main purpose being to provide background information relevant to official policy decisions."[3] Thus the invitation for scientific input into the policy decisions of UNCHE was clearly (and necessarily) hedged. And the line was sharply drawn between the function of the scientist and that of the politician.

Such sharp distinctions, however, are the invention of the very consciousness that, having gotten us into the present mess, needs somehow to be altered if we are to find our way out of it. They follow from a mechanistic mode of thought which conceives of the world in terms of distinct

[3] Barbara Ward and René Dubos, *Only One Earth: The Care and Maintenance of a Small Planet* (New York: W. W. Norton, 1972), p. viii.

parts, separable functions, and orderly processes of cause
and effect. When we perceive the world as whole system, we
must throw out some of this orderliness. It's messy to admit
that everything is connected to everything else, but the perception corresponds more nearly, we discover, with experience. Professional politicians are limited by their special
narrow interests, their biases and blindnesses, just as scientists are by theirs. The solution is clearly not to transfer
the power of decision-making from politician to scientist. In
large measure, that mistake has already been made; technocracy has proven as disastrous to the environment as
unbridled capitalism. These decisions, on which the survival
and the quality of life of the entire human species depend,
cannot be the exclusive domain of either the politicians or
the scientists.

It was the realization that, even allowing for scientific
"input," its very structure and makeup would make it impossible for the United Nations really to come to grips with
many of the critical issues of survival that led Alfred Hassler
to propose to the Menton biologists after their presentation
at the U.N. that Dai Dong sponsor an independent conference in Stockholm to coincide with UNCHE. The idea was
not to picket the U.N., or to stage a counterconference, but
to highlight the inadequacies of UNCHE through a parallel
conference of experts not beholden to their national governments. As a Dai Dong brochure put it: "Not anti-UN or
opposed to the UN Conference, the Independent Conference will seek to demonstrate the difficulties of dealing with
environmental problems through a world agency to which
individual nations refuse to relinquish sovereignty. It will
examine the social, economic and political origins of the
environmental crisis, and it can emphasize the need for
global solutions that will transcend national and corporate
interests."

"We've been asked repeatedly by journalists and
others," Hassler would tell the opening plenary of the Independent Conference, "whether Dai Dong is hostile to the
U.N., or whether we're in competition with the U.N. Conference. What we want is what the U.N. Conference is

supposed to be, but we want a great deal more than it is. We are hammering an alarm gong to the public to say, 'It is good that there is a U.N. Conference, but do not be satisfied.' We need a great deal more."

The biologists reacted favorably to the idea of an independent meeting, and the Dai Dong staff, in the United States under the direction of Alfred Hassler, and in Europe under the direction of Jens Brøndum, went to work planning the conference structure, drawing up a list of possible participants, and making the practical arrangements in Sweden. The conference would be divided into four work groups, each assigned to a broad problem area—environment and development, political and social structures, security and war, and ideology.

The UNCHE draft declaration issued in early spring, 1972, had stated flatly: "There is no fundamental conflict between economic . . . development and the preservation and enhancement of the human environment, since both seek to provide and sustain increasing opportunities to all peoples for a better life." This is at the very least a questionable proposition. The catch is in the key phrase, "human environment," borrowed from the title of the conference. It's not clear what the phrase actually means. Environment is, as its etymology indicates, that which *encircles*, or surrounds. But why modify *environment* with *human*? One possibility is that *human* environment consists of humanity, and is thus distinguished from the environment that surrounds humans—air, earth, and water. This, at least, was the meaning intended by a ruddy, rawboned member of the Hog Farm commune, his straight, blond hair gathered into a ponytail, who asked at Dai Dong's opening press conference whether the Dai Dong meeting would talk about the *inner* environment—from the skin in, he clarified. He got a blank stare by way of answer from the bemused Jens Brøndum. Anyway, this was surely not the meaning intended by either the namers of UNCHE or the framers of the document, in which the modification of *environment* with *human* seems superfluous, if not downright nonsensical. For the environment that surrounds humans also surrounds everything else. This is why the draft declaration prepared for the Dai Dong Independent Conference began by countering, "It is not a human environment, but an environment of which humans are a part." A critical point, because the truth is that the phrase is neither superfluous nor even casual, but is rather a calculated solipsism: the *human* environment is the environment seen through human eyes, and valued in terms of human needs and desires.

To some extent this is proper. Human beings are human beings, after all, not giraffes, or whales, or walnut trees. Our own eyes, our own values are the only ones we've got. Solipsism is inevitable—even healthy. But science has been based (like all social and technological development, which is interdependent with science) on man's ability, unique among living things, to project his perception imaginatively beyond himself, so that his subjective perception is counterpoised by a theoretical, objective one. Solipsism is neither false nor wicked, but human progress depends on the more or less constant exertion of an intellectual counterforce.

The U.N.'s notion of a human environment is an opportunistic acquiescence to *mere* solipsism. The *human* environment is clearly whatever humans say it is, and that gets us off the hook of responsibility to the rest of creation. If the human environment is whatever we say it is, and if the *human* environment is the only one that matters, then we are freed from the obligation to bring into accord what we wish to be true with what science tells us is objectively true. We need to worry about the environment of whales, for instance, only insofar as it impinges on our human interests. The questions are merely, what do we want from whales, and how can we most conveniently get it? There is a terrible presumptuousness in this attitude. We are fond of making a fable of the dinosaurs, who "died out," it is said, because they hadn't the brains to adjust to a changing environment. The poor, fusty things are held up as an example to children that brains, not brawn, determine survival, and man congratulates himself on his superior mental powers. Yet the fact is that the age of the dinosaurs lasted

150 million years, while in a scant million[4] man has woven the fabric of his own demise.

The human solipsism, not balanced by a complementary, scientific objectivity, is presumptuous in a special way. Other living things modify their environments unconsciously, according to genetic dictates; they arrive at a relation of equilibrium with their environment as naturally as water finds its own level.[5] In the vast majority of instances, organisms do not alter their environment in fulfilling their genetic program. Even in the rare instances in which they do (such as the overgrazing of grasslands, or the primeval production of atmospheric oxygen by oceanic plants and microorganisms, which provided the chemical environment necessary for the evolution of animal life), their unconscious nature places them beyond (or short of) what we may call value. Human consciousness, on the other hand, burdens man with moral choice. Since the industrial revolution, his capacity for making alterations in the global environment has grown exponentially—infinitesimally at first, by now at a terrifying speed. Everyday decisions of modern government and industry have global consequences. This explosion of technological power has seduced man with the illusion of absolute power, the dream of the genie in the magic lamp. But the earth (we must come back, again and again, to this) is a single system. The fate of each organism is connected to the fate of every other organism. Technological man, intoxicated by his own wizardry, has ignored this interdependence of living things and vital elements.

But not only does he contemptuously ignore the fact that the environment belongs equally to species other than

---

[4] Recent archaeological discoveries in Africa may show that this long-accepted estimate of man's age should be doubled.

[5] In the long run, there is no such thing as a steady-state in nature; the whole system of the earth, of the universe, is inexorably changing. The concept of ecological equilibrium is thus approximate and relative. It is nevertheless a useful ideal against which to measure the quality of man's relationship with his environment in the here-and-now and the foreseeable future. "In the long run," quipped Keynes economically, "we are all dead."

his own, in fact man has not even species loyalty. Greed and fear and ambition move him to act against the interests of his own species often more horribly than against others. He exploits and murders segments of his own human population, and assures the misery, perhaps the total destruction of future generations. For all his mental superiority, he is remarkably shortsighted in his egoism, and he is remarkably wicked. The moral aspect of the environmental problem is crucial. Science tells us loudly and unequivocally the outrageous risks of continuing to exploit and pollute the fragile planetary system. There is no way to understand our continued dalliance with disaster except to admit it to be a failure of morality, not primarily one of reason. Man the toolmaker, the maker of language, of civilization, is not too stupid to grasp what his own invention, science, tells him; man must understand that the global crisis has not come about through honest mistakes.

In this light the U.N. statement is patently false. There *is* a fundamental conflict between economic development and the preservation and enhancement of the whole environment. Economic development means the extraction and exploitation of the earth's resources. It means the construction of factories which must inevitably discharge substances that degrade the environment. The conflict is clear and simple and fundamental, and only by facing it can we hope to resolve it satisfactorily. It is this fundamental conflict between development and environmental stability that the first of the Dai Dong work groups was to consider. The question is particularly critical in view of the desperate and legitimate need for economic development in third-world countries. The UNCHE strategy of pretending ostrich-like that the conflict does not exist will not make it go away.

This wishful thinking of UNCHE is all the worse for being, at bottom, disingenuous. The UNCHE delegates were not blue-eyed Pollyannas, for the most part, but savvy international politicians, whose disregard of the conflict was willful. To put the most favorable construction on it, we could call it misguided diplomacy. More cynical constructions suggest themselves. The same quality characterizes

the report of the UNCHE preparatory conference at
Founex in 1971, a gathering of twenty-seven professionals
in the fields of economics and planning, commissioned by
Maurice Strong to formulate the problematic relationship
between environment and development in third-world countries. The Founex Report was issued by UNCHE as its
major background document in this area. The underlying weakness of the report is its failure to confront the
human roots of the environmental crisis, except insofar as
these roots consist in occasional oversight and miscalcula-
tion. To read this paper, one would never think that conflict
often arises as the result of intentional exploitation or con-
tradictory values.

"The Founex Report showed that although conflicts
between development and environment may arise, they are
not necessarily inevitable or inescapable and that through
proper planning developmental and environmental measures can be harmonized in such a way that they become
mutually supporting," the accompanying report by
UNCHE's secretary-general coolly states.[6] The report is
quite pervaded by a puzzling optimism about the willingness
of just about everyone to get together to solve these problems.
The secretary-general writes that "the interest of developing
countries in the environmental issue derives [among two
other 'basic factors' from the fact that] they share the concern of all mankind for the preservation and care of the
common resources of the oceans and the atmosphere."
Brazil's open invitation to developed nations to export their
most heavily polluting industries to her virgin jungle, which
still has (her representatives claimed) the capacity to
absorb their wastes, was only the crassest demonstration that
all mankind is far from sharing the concern mentioned by
Maurice Strong, least of all those in a position to do something about it. Those of us who were in Stockholm had a
chance to see the horribly disfigured and crippled victims
of indiscriminate industrial dumping of mercury wastes into
Minamata Bay in Japan. The twisted fingers and limbs,

[6] "Development and Environment," U.N., Doc. A/CONF.48/10, p. 2.

the contorted, imbecilic faces of these men and women and children, poisoned by the shellfish from their bay, didn't instill optimism over mankind's concern for anything other than expanding profits. The other side of the same coin is that the one-half or so of humanity that lives in a constant state of hunger and malnutrition (that lives, as Yusuf Eraj put it emphatically at the Dai Dong Conference, a sub-human existence) is in no condition to share Strong's environmental concern, which is unimaginably remote from the grinding, day-to-day struggle for mere survival. How can a man who is starving worry about anything but food?

Blithely, Strong goes on, "the problem is basically one of devising a pattern of development in which environmental objectives go hand in hand with economic, social and cultural goals, of identifying and acting upon the complementarities rather than the conflicts between multiple objectives." Perhaps we ought at least to be warned that to devise such a pattern of development is merely to fly in the face of all previous economic (which is to say human) history. It must be done if we are going to survive, but let us say frankly that this is a call for revolution, for a radical restructuring of society and government, and more basically still, for a radical shift in human motivation. Yet nowhere does the Founex Report (or any other UNCHE document, for that matter) recognize that the solutions demanded by the global crisis must be revolutionary. And for good reason. The United Nations serves the governments of which it is composed, and not many of those governments are in the business of revolution. Quite simply, the U.N. is not in a position to tell the developing nations, which comprise most of its membership, to cool their ardor for polluting development, nor is it in a position to tell the industrialized nations, which provide most of its money and power, to consume less and live more modestly in order to share their wealth with the poor. Each nation comes with its own interests to protect and advance, crippling the U.N. with this profound contradiction: in order to hold together at all, the U.N. is obliged to serve precisely those parochial national interests that its structure was intended to transcend. A cynic at the Dai Dong Conference remarked that the U.N. is the least.the governments can get away with. The recommendations of the Founex Report for "policy action" are thus predictably watery and conventional. The reality is that, so long as conventional solutions are pursued, even running as hard as they can, the impoverished nations of the world can only fall further and further behind the rich.

The need for revolutionary social and political structures was to be the focus of a second work group of the Dai Dong Conference. The structures through which the world has come to the brink of disaster, it seemed clear, must be abandoned or at least radically altered. Dai Dong offers no specific political program for change; it sees its role as persuading people of the necessity for change. But it espouses one fundamental idea, that only solutions that are transnational, not merely international, can avert the catastrophe looming ahead. A variety of political structures have emerged and flourished throughout human history, many of which have worked well through phases of the evolution of human cultures. Others of course have not worked so well. But at this juncture of history we are all in trouble, no matter what political structure we live in, because the trouble we are in transcends political boundaries. There is token recognition of this in the UNCHE motto, "Only One Earth." Yet the United Nations is itself a club of nations. Each nation comes at best with the intention of engaging in "international cooperation," yet never calling into question the concept of national sovereignty in which it clothes its interests.

Sovereignty is a legal concept developed in the Middle Ages at a time when, in the context of the feudal system, political entities were virtually self-sufficient. The feudal system was a hierarchy of contractual relationships in which those lower in the social pyramid pledged service and allegiance to those above in exchange for social order and protection from enemies. Even then, no magic protected sovereignty. If a baron who was more powerful than his neighbor decided to attack him, his neighbor's claim of sovereignty didn't help much. The development of money

economy and world trade in the late Middle Ages began
the outmoding of the concept of sovereignty, which was,
after all, even when it described political reality fairly well,
only an intellectual construct, never a substantial reality.
In the second half of the twentieth century, with our global
wars, our giant multinational corporations, and our global
pollution, which drifts across political frontiers into the common atmosphere and the oceans, not to mention the insanity
of weapons that threaten to blow up the planet, the fiction
of national sovereignty has no more applicability than the
divine right of kings. It simply does not describe reality
as we experience it. Worse, the appeal to national sovereignty is a folly that stands in the way of global community,
and is thus a deadly game the world can ill afford to play.

Maurice Strong recognized the inadequacies of present
concepts of sovereignty in dealing with global problems,
although he hedged his remarks to the opening plenary session of UNCHE first by equivocating with the word *sovereignty* itself, and second by putting off formal debate and
action to a comfortably indefinite future. "Beyond Stockholm," he asked the conference, "what kind of an edifice
must we build on the foundations we will be constructing
here? I believe we must build on these foundations new
concepts of sovereignty based not on the surrender of
national sovereignties, but on better means of exercising
those sovereignties collectively and with a greater sense of
responsibility for the common good. . . . The dominant
image of the age in which we live is that of the earth rising
above the horizon of the moon—a beautiful, solitary,
fragile sphere which provides the home and sustains the
life of the entire human species. From this perspective it is
impossible to see the boundaries of nations and all the other
artificial barriers that divide men. . . . Our common dependence on the health of our only one earth and our common
interest in caring for it transcend all our man-made divisions. . . . In the decades ahead, we must learn to conquer
our own divisions, our greeds, our inhibitions, and our fears.
Or they will conquer us."

Early in this century, the idea of internationalism was

a progressive one. In the spirit of internationalism, the first steps toward global cooperation were taken, notable among them the creation of the League of Nations. Ernst Winter, founder and director of the Transnational Research Center in Austria, says he coined the word *transnational*. "Why? Because we felt when we did this ten years ago," he explained, "that the international world needs a complement to itself; the international world has stabilized to mean *member states*, a club of governments. It no longer means what it used to mean to our parents and grandparents—the vision of one mankind, of all nations being brothers, of all peoples working together. That concept is still in the minds of many. There are about thirty-two thousand organizations that use the word *international* in their title—the International Pigeon Raisers' Association. Obviously, there's not one government representative in there. These people think that everybody who raises homing pigeons should cooperate, and be friends and brothers. But you see *international* no longer means that. And because it doesn't really mean that, these thirty-two thousand 'international' organizations are no longer really achieving what they think the term means. They have become quite isolated and ineffective. The term *transnational* takes the nation as an existing reality, but transcends it, and complements government. The world of tomorrow cannot be carried out simply by governments. It's impossible, totally impossible."

It is telling that a radical ideal of the period of internationalism was world government—essentially the concept of the nation state enlarged to encompass all existing states. If the world were one country with a single government, the reasoning went, international conflict could not arise. Many lessons of intervening history have taught the inadequacy of such a notion: political conflict cannot be resolved by further centralization of authority and power. We have seen the concentration of power result in gray bureaucracy, in the self-justifying juggernaut of the military-industrial complex, in tyranny and terror. The emergence of special interest groups and identities, from the black liberation movement in the U.S. to the nationalistic movements in former colonies throughout the third world, makes it clear that real solutions lie more in the direction of decentralization, of equal access to power and wealth for the world's people so that they can formulate their own values and govern their own destinies. At the same time, new global structures must be created in which locally autonomous communities can function and interact. More basically, new consciousness, new perceptions of the human predicament, need to be developed that transcend the narrow political interests of nation states in order to build a working global community.

A basic principle of ecology, the study of interrelationships within living systems, is that the more complex a system, the more stable it is. Although one cannot state the principle as a theorem, and debate and research continue about certain of its aspects, in essence the principle does describe how natural systems work. A commonly cited illustration is the hypothetical system in which a given organism preys not just on one but on several other species. In such a system, should the population of one prey species dwindle, or disappear altogether through an epidemic or other change in the system, the predator species has other prey species to fall back on, and is able to adjust to the altered environment. In a simpler system, where each link in the food chain is connected to only one predator species above and one prey species below, an epidemic in one species disrupts the entire system, and can bring on its collapse. The ways in which species diversity enhances the stability of ecosystems are more complex than this model, and vary considerably. But in general it can be said that diversity gives a system flexibility. Genetic diversity within a species functions in the same way, protecting it with adaptability to fluctuations in the conditions of its environment.

A corollary principle would state the danger of concentration in any single area or aspect of a system. In the case of the predator, specialization on a single prey species is risky. In general parlance we say you shouldn't put your eggs in just one basket. An investor who risks everything on a single stock stands to make his fortune, but he is also liable to lose his shirt. The diversified portfolio may show less spectacular returns, but it is correspondingly safer.

> My ventures are not in one bottom trusted,
> Nor to one place; nor is my whole estate
> Upon the fortune of this present year:
> Therefore my merchandise makes me not sad,

says Antonio confidently in *The Merchant of Venice*. This is a tricky principle, however, because concentration, while it may be risky, is efficient, and human progress (real as well as dubious) thrives on efficiency. The industrial revolution was based on the invention of the factory, for example, which was simply putting into operation the efficiency of concentrated power. The problem is that the same efficiency that powered all the machines in the factory from a single source, and had each human laborer singlemindedly inserting the same part or tightening the same screw at his invariable station on the assembly line, just as efficiently concentrated the polluting effluents of manufacture, concentrated poverty and disease and misery in the ghettos it constructed for its workers, and concentrated the smoldering rage of the exploited and oppressed as a lens gathers sunlight into a point of fire. As Marx foresaw, the cruel factory system of the early nineteenth century built into itself the mechanism of its own undoing. By concentrating workers into the factory, the owners unwittingly brought them into organizations that ultimately rose to challenge the owners' power. In the long run, the factory system was forced by the unions that inevitably grew up within its walls to adjust to the demands of workers for decent wages and working conditions. But this self-adjustment permitted the factory system to continue growing, and growth in turn depended on ever-greater concentration, even as corporations expanded their operations. For corporate expansion leads, paradoxically, not to diffusion but to concentration.

With the concentration demanded by corporate manufacture came growing urbanization, for it is highly efficient for the efficient factories to concentrate themselves around hubs of transportation, and around populous urban centers;

this concentration decreases the costs of distribution while it draws more people into the industrial centers from their distant and scattered and inefficient villages and farms, in turn creating a larger work force to produce the additional consumer goods permitted by all this efficiency and demanded by the expanding population, and so on, round and round the carousel of ever-expanding profits and pollution.

Any local environment, being itself finite, has a finite carrying capacity for pollutants. It can absorb, break down, and detoxify only a certain amount of material in a given time period. When the environment is burdened beyond its carrying capacity, it degrades, sometimes irreversibly. The effluents of a given population, distributed more or less evenly throughout a given land area, may be well within the total environment's carrying capacity. But if the population is concentrated into a few centers, the local environments of these centers must absorb a higher proportion of the overall pollution. The higher the concentration of the population, the more its level of pollution approaches the carrying capacity of the local environment, until at some point it surpasses it. This is one of the obvious drawbacks of cities. Organic sewage, which when properly distributed forms valuable fertilizer that revitalizes the earth with its nutrients, becomes in urban concentrations poisonous waste.

Modern animal husbandry is similarly plagued with concentration. Cattle, for instance, are no longer grazed on open lands where their wastes return to the earth many of the nutrients the animals take from it. Instead, it has been found more efficient to bring them together in feedlots— giant complexes of crowded pens where the animals are fed grain grown far away on chemical fertilizers, necessitated by the absence of the animals and their manure. The concentration of the animals, in turn, transforms their once valuable manure into poison that must be washed away, and usually ends up as pollutant runoff in streams and rivers. The faster buck turned by this efficiency for the merchants of meat is in reality purchased at an enormous and spiraling, although invisible cost to the general environment and the public health.

The problem of feedlots parallels the general trend in agriculture toward concentration in monoculture. In all managed agriculture "man intentionally reduces the diversity of a natural system in order to maximize the production of one or a few components."[7] When large areas of farmland are used to produce a single crop, this effect is multiplied, and nutrients which might have been replaced by crop rotation are lost from the soil and have to be replaced by ever-increasing applications of chemical fertilizers, resulting in ever-increasing runoff of the chemicals into streams and rivers. The amount of runoff is compounded by the exponential loss in efficiency of increasing applications of fertilizer, since the greater the application, the lower the proportion actually taken up by the plants. Thus, to achieve a constant yield from his acreage, the farmer must use more and more fertilizer. And the more he uses, the higher the proportion leached.

Yet another aspect of concentration is the psychologically deadening standardization that accompanies the development of industrial society. The developer levels the troublesomely varied countryside with powerful bulldozers and covers it efficiently with identical "homes," or with complexes of high-rise honeycombs. High-speed mass production, which is based on the interchangeability of parts, is the real model for contemporary industrial society. The extended family with its individuality, its quirks and ties, has had to give way, it is said, to modern mobility. But this vaunted mobility is in fact mere interchangeability. The corporate executive transfered from Bridgeport to Tulsa suffers no more disorientation in his new environment than a universal joint in one Ford or another. He phones his wife one afternoon to break the news, she phones a moving company the next, and within a month she is reinstalled in another fully applianced, enamel-and-formica Early American kitchen, and he is commuting as he always has over

[7] *Man in the Living Environment: A Report on Global Ecological Problems* (Madison, Wis.: Institute of Ecology, 1972), p. 117.

traffic-clogged expressways to his ulcerous work. He indulges in uniform flirtations with isomorphic secretaries. She cultivates her infidelities as predictably as her shrubs. No purple mountains' majesty above the fruited plain—America has become a pastel, slightly pliable, uniform mass, in which identical particles trade places, only their speed rising and falling with the fluctuating heat of the economy.

It is equally deadening to apply generalized techniques and solutions to varying agricultural conditions. The ecology of a local system, even a system that through cultivation has been relatively simplified, is so complex that generalizations formulated in one context are not reliable to deal with the intricate interrelationships within another. Each situation must be analyzed and dealt with individually if well-intentioned intervention is not to lead to disaster. The difficulty (not to say danger) of applying standardized agricultural techniques is illustrated in the exportation of techniques developed in the North Temperate Zone to the tropics. One of the drawbacks of chemical pesticides, even in the North Temperate Zone, is that they often destroy many harmless species along with the target species, and thus reduce the diversity of the agricultural system. This problem is intensified in the tropics, where climate is more favorable year-round, and the pests produce many more generations per year, on the one hand requiring greater and more frequent applications of pesticide, on the other hand greatly increasing the probability of the development of resistant strains. Most of the herbicides developed for the temperate zones have proved rather ineffective in the tropics, the heavy rainfall further reducing their usefulness by diluting them (and washing them away from the site of application, adding the problem of pollution through runoff).

Tropical soil presents another problem. Jungle systems are obviously extremely productive, but their soils contain surprisingly small amounts of organic material, and their lush growth depends on the continual redepositing of decaying vegetation on the jungle floor. Bacteria, molds, insects, and other invertebrate animals consume the organic debris almost immediately. When the jungle trees are cleared in order to cultivate the land, the organic material in the soil disappears in about a year, and the mineral nutrients necessary for the growth of plants are washed away by the heavy tropical rains which beat down on the unprotected soil. The intense tropical sun quickly bakes the nutrient-poor clay that remains into a brick-hard, sterile wasteland, a process called laterization. Even jungle vegetation has difficulty reestablishing itself on laterized soil; usually tough grasses invade the area, precluding the return of original plant forms. The process of laterization is not well understood, and much research and modification of existing agricultural techniques must precede the widespread development of modern agriculture in the tropics.

Like the generalized approach to a multiplicity of agricultural situations, the single-thrust solution to environmental problems usually carries with it an entire complex of new and unforeseen complications. Perhaps the most notorious instance is the indiscriminate application of DDT to control insect pests. When it was first developed, DDT seemed a miracle. Indeed, by controlling the mosquito that carries malaria, the chemical has virtually eliminated the disease from many areas of the world, and drastically reduced its occurrence in others. But now we know that its use has produced DDT-resistant strains of the very pests and disease-carriers it was meant to eradicate. In Guatemala, for instance, where an intensive malaria eradication program based on heavy application of a variety of chemical insecticides including DDT was instituted twelve years ago, the mosquitoes have become resistant, and the incidence of the disease is higher than before the start of the program. At the same time, samples of mothers' milk contain the highest levels of DDT reported anywhere in the world, several hundred times the acceptable level set by the World Health Organization.[8] Because DDT (like the other

[8] Commoner, *Closing Circle*, p. 247; also cited in Harrison Wellford, *Sowing the Wind* (New York: Grossman Publishers, 1972), pp. 265–266.

chlorinated hydrocarbons) is a persistent chemical—that is, it does not readily break down in the environment—it becomes concentrated in the food chain and is distributed across the globe. DDT has been found in significant concentrations in the fatty tissues of antarctic penguins, living thousands of miles from any area of application. The peregrine falcon faces almost certain extinction because the DDT in the system of the female birds produces egg shells too soft to incubate. The long-term genetic effects of DDT in other species, including man, are still largely undetermined.

The difficulty is that much of agriculture has seemed to lock itself into economic dependence on such chemicals—if not the persistent chlorinated hydrocarbons with their long-term hazards, then the potent organophosphates and carbamates with their lethal short-term hazards—so that discontinuing their use appears to entail hardships greater than those of continued use. The truth is, however, that exclusive dependence on chemical pesticides is a folly promoted by the chemical companies in spite of the fact that it leads inevitably to diminishing returns for the farmer as it poses ever-greater threats to the environment. "Pesticide chemicals have clearly played a major role in the development of present agricultural abundance," writes Harrison Wellford in *Sowing the Wind*:

> Yet their early success instilled a technological arrogance which led many farmers to abandon natural controls and rely exclusively on chemicals to protect their crops. In putting all their eggs in one technological basket, they perilously ignored the adaptability and genetic diversity of their insect enemies. There is now compelling evidence that the single strategy of chemical control has been an economic as well as environmental failure. Although insecticide use increased nearly 150 percent between 1957 and 1967, there are now more insect species of pest status than ever before; many of the most harmful pests have developed resistance to chemicals; the use of ever more indiscriminantly toxic pesticides has destroyed the pests' natural enemies; and

the costs of pest control for many farmers have mush-
roomed to the point of diminishing returns.[9]

The solution is not, as many environmentalists urge, to
abandon the use of chemical pesticides altogether, Wellford
concludes. "The reformers," he contends, fail "to recognize
that pesticides, when used as ecologically selective tools,
are often necessary in helping to maintain the balance of
some insect populations." Instead, Wellford advocates a
multiple-thrust solution to what is in every case an intricate
complex of problems, not simply a pest that needs to be
gotten rid of. He calls this strategy "integrated control."
"With this system, farmers do not rely exclusively on chemicals to sterilize their fields of all insect life, but use a variety
of biological, cultural, mechanical, and chemical controls to
manipulate insect populations until they reach a healthy
pest-predator balance. They use pesticides only after other
measures fail to prevent crop damage and then only use
pesticides which are most specific for the pest in the smallest
possible amounts."[10] Integrated control is thus a system of
human intervention that mimics the complexity and interdependence of the natural environment in which it intervenes.

In the production of energy, too, concentration and
generalization present us with enormous problems. Many
people, conscious that the internal-combustion engine
accounts for a major portion of urban air pollution, look to
the electrification of cars and buses as a solution. Yet this
solution, while it may bring about some overall reduction
in air pollution, moves the pollution from the individual
vehicle and concentrates it at the generating plant (which
is required to charge batteries and to power trolleys),
where it adds a huge burden to the already overtaxed supply
of electrical energy. If we imagine that nuclear-powered
generating plants will save us from both the scarcity of
power and the air pollution of conventional generating
methods, we are at once confronted with the enormous and

[9] *Sowing the Wind*, p. 239.
[10] Ibid., pp. 256, 276.

escalating danger of radiation leakage from the plants themselves as well as exposure from radioactive wastes. In addition to the danger of radiation, nuclear power plants cause
thermal pollution of the rivers into which they return the
water they have used to cool their generators, often disas-
trously changing their ecology. Stick your finger in one hole
in the dike, and the water spurts through in ten others.

The principle holds just as true on the political level.
The "green revolution" is looked to as the solution to the
worldwide problem of hunger. The term green revolution
refers to the recent development of hybrid seed strains
which, in combination with irrigation, mechanization, and
large applications of chemical fertilizers and pesticides,
produce much higher yields than traditional strains. The
crucial biological development was the genetic dwarfing of
the plants' stalks, which could not ordinarily support the
weight of the increased yields induced by massive doses
of fertilizer. The yields of these grains are indeed impressive. Moreover, the solution to the problem of hunger, as
we have noted earlier, is necessarily prior to enhancement
of the environment in third-world countries. It is also prior
to more general economic development. And development
is in turn the way for these countries to become politically
independent, productively functioning members of the
world community. Yet the contradictions are painfully
obvious. There seems no alternative to the green revolution
as a means to produce the exponentially expanding require-
ment for food in the third world, and in fact it is very much
under way in many countries. But the green revolution
brings with it a mind-boggling web of consequences. Local,
usually varied agriculture must be turned to monoculture,
which, with its specialization in a single grain, carries the
threat of malnutrition even as it relieves hunger. Draft
animals, who take their energy from the virtually inexhaust-
ible source of the sun, and who return the nutrients they
take from the soil in their manure, must be replaced by
machinery, which is made from and consumes nonrenewable resources, and whose manufacture and operation are
polluting. Dams must be built for irrigation, which seriously

and usually irreversibly alter the local environment and provide breeding grounds for disease. Increasing use of chemical fertilizers and pesticides means increasing pollution of waters, poisoning of the food chain, and destruction of beneficial species. The "rationalization" of agriculture requires the conglomeration of land and increasing concentration of population in urban centers to serve the expanding industrial base needed to support mechanized agriculture. There are political consequences as well. Adoption of the green revolution in third-world countries increases their political and economic dependence on the industrialized countries who control the technology and the manufacture of the chemicals and machinery, the very countries whose domination they wish to escape. Another hopelessly vicious cycle.

It is not hard to see why single-thrust interventions in the environment often create more problems than they solve —why the dike springs ten leaks for every hole you plug. In a system as complex as even a local environment, relationships are not linear. A schematic illustration of such a system would show rather each element of the system as a hub from which lines representing multiple relationships radiate to the other elements. Directly or indirectly, each element in a system is connected to every other element, and each element is potentially affected by modification in another. It is a basic principle of ecology that a system can be dealt with successfully only on the level of the bounds of that system. A problem locally within a system, in other words, cannot be treated in isolation from the rest of the system. By the same token, the complexity of a solution must be equal to the complexity of the system it is designed to treat. Systems problems do not yield to simplistic, single-thrust solutions. There are no magic buttons in a system, no keystones that control the behavior of the whole system. You cannot hope to discover the one critical center around which everything falls into place. In a system, there is no main problem.

Failure to acknowledge this complexity is the critical weakness of the controversial report of the computer analysis of the global crisis, *The Limits to Growth*.[11] The research, carried out at the Massachusetts Institute of Technology under the sponsorship of the Club of Rome, was based on a computer model of world dynamics in terms of five critical parameters which were judged to be reliable indices of the global system: pollution, depletion of resources, economic growth, population growth, and quality of life measured as the level of consumption. The researchers made a variety of theoretical assumptions about future levels of these parameters, and received a variety of readouts which expressed the putative scenarios graphically. What would happen, for instance, if current rates for all other parameters continued, but population leveled off? If technology solved the problems of pollution and resource depletion that accompany economic growth? If new discoveries of nonrenewable resources doubled present known stocks? Every program ended in collapse within a hundred years except the program that assumed a leveling off of economic growth. The researchers concluded that only by stopping growth could the looming global catastrophe be averted.

The Club of Rome's report has been attacked for a variety of reasons. *The New York Times Book Review* attacked its data, citing the classic dictum of the computer scientists, "garbage in, garbage out." An eminent economist told me bluntly it was bad science, "beneath contempt." Others have attacked the authors as prophets of doom and gloom; technology, they insist, will get us out of the crisis as surely as it has gotten us into it. *The Limits to Growth*, they say, has no more credibility as a prediction of the future than the prophet who warned before the appearance of the automobile that we would by now be up to our necks in horse-shit. These criticisms avoid confronting the main point, that we are in a hell of a fix and had better do something about it, instead of sitting back and waiting for the technological cavalry to arrive in the nick of time to save us.

[11] Donella H. Meadows et al., *Limits to Growth: A Report for the Club of Rome's Project on the Predicament of Mankind* (New York: Universe Books, 1972).

The Limits to Growth does not pretend to be futurology, and it makes this disclaimer repeatedly. It is quite obvious that since it projects many different theoretical futures, it cannot possibly be predicting a real one. To belabor the study on this ground is to flay not a dead horse, but one that never existed. The report merely offers graphic representations of current, actual rates of growth and consumption extended into a theoretical future, a few hypothetical variations on that theme, and a discussion of the implications of those facts and extrapolations.

The real weakness of the report is not its failure to predict the future accurately (which it doesn't claim to do), but its reductive approach to the problem. Stop growth, it says, and the rest of the system will proceed in Prussian cause-and-effect orderliness toward healthy equilibrium. But everything we know about systems tells us that this cannot be true. Only multiple solutions that deal simultaneously with all the problems—unchecked industrial growth, unchecked population growth, resource depletion, pollution, hunger, and, if you will, "quality of life," measured by far more complex indices than merely the level of consumption—will prevent the collapse of the global system, which *The Limits to Growth* correctly perceives to be a threat.

Moreover, the fallacy of searching for single critical solutions to complex global problems—focusing on growth alone—has rather sinister political implications. It is a coincidence perhaps not without significance that the Club of Rome is a highly elite organization, limited to one hundred industrialists, scientists, and economists who have joined in the recognition that the industrial system, coupled with population growth, is bringing the world quickly to the brink of disaster. Aurelio Peccei, founder of the Club of Rome and vice-chairman of Fiat, for example, is a man accustomed to sitting at the apex of a substantial hierarchy of power, making decisions that have predictable repercussions downward throughout the entire, well-oiled corporate machine. It is of course admirable and fortunate that men in positions of power such as Peccei recognize the danger, and recognize their own responsibility to do something about it. But it is worth noting that the very position from which he comes to the problem, the organizational structures in which he is used to working, might color Peccei's approach to solutions.

If the solution to the global predicament really can be reduced, as the Club of Rome's report suggests, to stopping economic growth, then (the implication seems to be) the efficient way to achieve this single objective is through the centralization of power. If one decision is to be made, it would be convenient for one man to make it. Democracy is inconvenient; bureaucracy is grindingly slow. A single enlightened dictator, counseled by a small staff of technicians, could best push the button that would save the world.

The dangers of concentration are just as real in the realm of politics as of pollution, not only because absolute power corrupts absolutely, but also because this conception fundamentally misconstrues the nature of the crisis. The environmental crisis is a crisis of politics as much as of pollution. Just as human intervention in ecosystems must be undertaken at the level of complexity of the whole system, patterns of political power ought to reflect the complexity of the social systems they govern. This means that as societies grow in complexity, political power needs to be decentralized, so that it reflects as nearly as possible the collective will—not just what daddy knows to be best. The fundamentally exploitative nature of the industrial system cannot be blithely ignored (as the U.N. tries to do) in the attempt to alter its course. In large part, the environmental crisis has reached its present proportions because political and economic power have been concentrated in the hands of the few at the expense of the many. To change this maldistribution of power means trouble, particularly at a time when the maintenance of the global environment requires more management, not less. And effective management is, as we have noted, made difficult by a diffusion of authority. Economist Herman Daly pointed out at Dai Dong's evaluative panel on the final day of UNCHE, that the political decentralization called for by most of the independent statements and declarations issued at Stockholm raises thorny economic problems. For most of the same statements and declarations also condemned the decentralized, "free" market economy, fucled by the profit motive. The question is: how can decentralized decision-making effectively control the planned economy these independents were advocating? This apparent contradiction parallels Dai Dong's analysis of the paradox of the U.N.: the U.N.'s failure to be effective is seen as a function of its lack of centralized power, the result of the refusal of member states to relinquish sovereignty to it.

The solution to this paradox lies in the development of structures of authority that are centralized in that they embody the overall connections among disparate elements of the community and consist of clear channels of communication and feedback among them, but which derive their authority from the multiplicity of inputs from their entire constituency—genuine inputs, which actually determine and modify policy. Simply, power ought not to be thought to reside in authority structures conceived as separate from the people whom those structures govern, or thought to be wielded by the powerful over the powerless. Rather, power —the ability to effect or forestall change—ought to be seen as distributed through all levels of society, so that those who govern take their legitimacy from those they govern. This seems utopian, yet there is no obvious reason why political structures should not mimic the structures of the ecosystems in which they operate—incredibly various and complex, yet whole, and (*mirabile dictu*) efficient. The revolution isn't going to come about by making the bullies now in power act nicer to people, of course. The people themselves have to stop preferring being bullied to taking responsibility for their own destinies. Power cannot be given to people; it can only come from them. This objective of decentralization of power, of multiple approaches to complex problems, of turning away from concentration and generalization, is what characterizes the underlying philosophical distinction between the old, internationalist ideal of world government, and Dai Dong's vision of a transnational global community.

Structures, however, no matter how perfectly devised,

do not in themselves solve political problems. No clearer
example could be found of the inadequacy of structure
alone to assure political justice and stability than the seizing
of inordinate power by the executive branch of the U.S.
government, most heinously in its destruction of Southeast
Asia, and in the impotence of Congress to restore the balance of constitutional power. An equivalent example is the
betrayal of the Russian Revolution by bureaucracy. Among
the greatest obstacles to world community is the ideological
division that sets people against one another in hopelessly
bitter struggle. It was this problem of ideology to which a
third of the work groups of the Dai Dong Conference was to
direct its attention.

On the one hand, the environmental crisis that con-
fronts the globe transcends ideology. The entire human
species faces famine, poisoning, and, finally, extinction. If
the crazed holders to one ideology decide to launch a
nuclear war, no one else's ideology, however enlightened,
is going to save him from the apocalypse. Developed socialist and capitalist countries alike are choked by air pollution
in their industrial centers, are poisoning their lakes and
rivers with sewage, chemical wastes, and runoff. Pollution
drifts across political borders as easily as it spreads within
them. The ozone layer threatened by supersonic flight pro-
tects Christian, Moslem, Jew, and devoutest unbeliever
from carcinogenic levels of solar radiation. In this light,
ideology seems silly, and quarreling over it seems petulant
and self-indulgent. If we are going to survive, we have to
see beyond our intellectual differences to our common
humanity and our common danger. We must transcend
ideology in order to confront reality.

On the other hand, the ideal of transcending ideology
is itself an ideology. This paradox was reflected in the work
group in an exchange between Frenchman André Faussurier, speaking through an interpreter, and French-Swiss
Jean Mussard, speaking an elegant, urbanely guttural English. Faussurier, putting his words together almost painfully, as though he were grappling with the whole serpentine
length of each thought, pointed out that the character of

ideology is to unify knowledge—to order reality within an overarching scheme that gives it meaning. And as it gives meaning to what is known, ideology is the source of meaning for the human being himself acting out his life in a particular social and historical context. But ideology, which functions productively so long as it gives meaning to life, comes to function negatively when it hardens into dogma.

In our own time, ideologies have come to seem actually opposed to what is known, to the system of scientific knowledge, and appear to be giving way to science and technology as determinants of policy and action. What in reality has happened is simply that science has become the new ideology, which may be called "scientism" and of which the technocrat is high priest. It is a mechanistic ideology, as well as an ideology of mechanism, which gives over ethical and aesthetic values in the name of what works, of what can be technically accomplished. Since it purports to be based on science rather than belief it is inflexible, and necessarily violent. The human being has become merely a token within the all-embracing and self-justifying technological system. It is the ideology of automated warfare, of the bulldozing and paving over of natural systems, of the reduction of human citizens to identification numbers and readouts from data banks and blips on screens.

The mechanistic ideology of "scientism" is necessarily violent because it is based on the abstracting and analytical methods of applied science. Analysis is taking things apart to get a better look at them; it leaves things in pieces. The analytical view of the universe is of a collection of particles. Analysis focuses on the particles in their isolation rather than on the relations that bind them together. We imagine we have replaced mystical and political ideologies with the rationalism of science, but our concept of rationality is dangerously narrow. What is needed now is a new ideology, based on scientific knowledge, but fundamentally relational rather than analytic, human in purpose and direction, and nonviolent. In the past, ideology has been imposed downward from the social and political hierarchy; the new ideology, if it is to be nonoppressive, must flow upward from the people. It must transcend the contemporary schism between ideology and science, and be the vehicle of synthesis of knowledge and values.

Faussurier's call for a new ideology was vigorously (though diplomatically) opposed by Jean Mussard. "I don't think that our task is to invent a new ideology," he said. "I don't even think that this is possible. I think that our task is to learn how to go beyond ideologies, to transcend the boundaries of ideologies." For Mussard, ideology is always and necessarily what Faussurier had distinguished as dogma. "To me an ideology is a crystalized system of thought, including moral principles and so on, which paralyzes us, of which we become prisoners, and which makes it impossible for us to see beyond certain concepts."

Perhaps the difficulty is resolved by shifting the focus of the argument. There is of course a definitional question. Faussurier's concept of ideology makes it an inescapable aspect of human consciousness; we inevitably fit the bits and pieces of experience into an overarching scheme of knowledge whether we are conscious of it or not. In this sense there is no transcending ideology—there is only exchanging one ideology for another. Mussard defines ideology as crystalized systems of thought, thus distinguishing ideology, presumably, from other systems of thought, which may not be crystalized and imprisoning. But let us accept Faussurier's definition, according to which ideology is necessary. Ideology then becomes dogma when it is pursued for its own sake, when the system of thought is treated as self-justifying in spite of advances in knowledge. Ideology ought instead to be seen to be as organic, something as fluent and protean as the living beings from which it springs. Furthermore, it must not be mistaken as an end in itself; it is a means to the fulfillment of human potential. Thus, ideology must not itself be pursued, or it will divert attention and energy from the real goals that need to be pursued. Moreover, it *need* not be pursued, since there is no escaping it. But an ideology must constantly be examined and modified in relation to the human situation it serves. Thus, if we accept Faussurier's definition, we can accept at the same time the thrust of Mussard's argument that a self-conscious concern with creating new ideology is misplaced energy.

Ideological conflict reaches its craziest, most suicidal pitch as war. "Throughout history," declared the Menton Statement,

> there has been no human activity so universally condemned and so universally practised as war, and research on ever more destructive weaponry and methods of warfare has been unremitting. . . . It is insufficient to attribute war to the natural belligerence of mankind. . . . In our time it is apparent that the dangers of global war focus at two points: 1.) the inequality that exists between industrialized and non-industrialized parts of the world, and the determination of millions of impoverished human beings to improve their lot; 2.) the competition for power and economic advantage among anarchic nation-states unwilling to relinquish selfish interests in order to create a more equitable society.

The problem facing the fourth of the work groups, whose central concern was war, is a double-edged sword: on the one hand, the total unacceptability of war as a method for solving conflict, on the other, the total unacceptability of oppression, and the legitimate need of oppressed people to struggle to be free. "Stated thus," the Menton document continued, "the problem seems almost insoluble. Yet mankind has demonstrated improbable resources of adaptability and resiliency in the past and perhaps facing what may well be the ultimate challenge to its survival, it will confound our fears once again."

II

Meeting Folks

A city bus runs the dozen miles from Stockholm's center to Graninge, the small retreat center where the Dai Dong Independent Conference was held. Or you could take a Volvo taxi if you were prepared to accept the environmental ironies and the stiff fare. Once past Nacka, a large center-less suburb of Stockholm, the highway winds through wooded, sparsely settled countryside; from a tiny bus shelter, you walk half a kilometer more up a dirt road to get to Graninge. It is an odd place, beautifully situated over a bay of the Baltic, but piously and austerely managed in the style of the Lutheran state church it is affiliated with. Half of each guest room is taken up by the two single bunks, virtuously hard and narrow, and fixed head to head against one wall, leaving space just wide enough to pass from door to window between the beds and the wash basin, wardrobe, and desk that line the opposite wall. Each guest is issued a cotton dish towel which is supposed to serve both for face and hands, and for the entire body after a shower—for which hot water is supplied between eight o'clock and nine each morning. The guest is also issued one airline-sized bar of soap which, like the dish towel, is to last him how-ever long he stays. The strategy, I guess, is to speed the guest on his way. Since the shower is furnished with hot water only one hour each morning, however, many guests find the soap ration adequate. In this protestant establish-ment at any rate, cleanliness isn't hard on the heels of godliness, but places well behind thrift in the moral order of things. Graninge is managed by a solemn Rotarian and his appropriately matronly wife, whose chief worry in life is the roguish disposition of their guests, for unspoken purposes, to steal the keys. Not a day of the conference went by without the Dai Dong staff's being closely questioned as to the whereabouts of Mister So-and-so's key, or Mister So-and-so's. Consequences were darkly hinted at, innuendoes let fall. The key conspiracy reached its most intense pitch, naturally, the last day of the conference, when every participant, down to the most honest-seeming, most eager-to-please gentleman with a tie, fell under suspicion of purposing to filch his key and disappear. These fears were not allayed by the fact that we were all but one *foreign* ladies and gentlemen.

But the place *was* lovely. In the bay sailboats moved silently about a large wooded island. Early in the sunny mornings I would run a few kilometers down the dirt road, winding through woods, then coming out among a cluster of summer houses on the water. Fishermen would be gathering their tackle and setting out in boats. A dog sleeping on a front porch woke and lifted his head to bark at me as I ran past. Beyond the houses there were horses in a dewy pasture, two chestnuts who stood and followed me with their eyes, and a white horse, stretched flat out on his side in the grass, who ignored me completely. I ran for a while behind a man riding to work on his bicycle through a field, my feet and my ankles quickly soaked from the dew on the tall grass, then turned back, past the dog again who was awake enough by now to give me a proper scolding at the very end of his straining tether. The first morning, I thought I'd cool off with a swim in the bay, and headed down to the water with quite a delicious anticipation. The deliciousness was short-lived, though. An algal bloom had turned the water slimy, and I thought better of jumping in. I muttered an imprecation or two on the irony, and trudged grudgingly up to the protestant showers instead.

The dirt road to Graninge was strewn, here and there, with beer cans, Yankee-style, but beer cans were conspicuously the only litter. Otherwise, the setting for Dai Dong's Independent Conference was idyllic. One of the staff, walking up the road from the bus stop early one evening, saw an unconcerned moose standing in an open field. And this idyllic quality, set apart from the traffic-bedeviled city with its official conference, was charmingly appropriate, though it was unplanned; for in fact, by the time Dai Dong's European staff came to making the conference arrangements, Graninge was the only place anywhere near Stockholm still able to accommodate such a gathering. The entire city had long since girt itself for an onslaught that in the end never quite materialized. Dai Dong did hire space in the center of town in the ABF House, the cultural building of the organization of Swedish labor unions This space was used for the press conferences, public meetings, and displays that made up the rest of its three-week program. The renting of ABF turned out to be something of a coup, actually, since other groups—notably the Swedish People's Forum—unable to find space of their own, appealed to Dai Dong for space in ABF. The programs of these other groups attracted their own constituencies and helped to make the ABF House one of the most important centers of independent conference activity in Stockholm.

The work groups of the Dai Dong Conference discovered quickly during their first session the morning of June first that they would have to focus their efforts on the declaration, which was to be made public at a press conference at ABF in less than a week, and which was to be read at Maurice Strong's invitation to the plenary session of UNCHE two days after that. The Dai Dong staff had prepared a draft declaration ahead of time for consideration by the conference. This had seemed an efficient way of proceeding in light of their experience at Menton, where the writing of the document from scratch proved to be an unnecessarily difficult business. Writing is hard in the best of circumstances; when half a dozen scientists try to write a statement together to which each will sign his name and which will be circulated among thousands of their colleagues, and when they have only a few days to do it, it is nearly impossible. So the American staff, principally Dorothy Maas and Alfred Hassler, prepared the draft and presented it to the March, 1972, meeting of the Dai Dong steering committee for approval. A few modifications were suggested and made at that time, but generally the steering committee thought the draft a good document that stated forcefully the problems of the environmental crisis and the weaknesses of UNCHE's approach to them.

The draft was written very much in response to the draft declaration prepared for UNCHE, which had been released earlier in the spring. Thus it stressed the refutation of certain assumptions and conclusions of the UNCHE document, and this slant, which tied it strongly to the final declaration UNCHE was expected to issue and gave it rather a reactive, or at best a counteroffensive tone, was perhaps the major source of dissatisfaction among the Dai Dong Conference participants. A crucial thorn was the draft's unequivocal condemnation of the concept of national sovereignty, which, to the staff's consternation, few of the participants were prepared to support. Each of the four work groups came quickly to consensus over the need for major revision—if not complete rewriting—of the proposed draft declaration, and it was on this task that they focused their attention.

Meanwhile, Stockholm prepared itself for the United Nations Conference, which was to begin in a week. Delegates arrived. Reporters and film crews wandered about, noses twitching for a story or a good shot. Each day brought more intense activity at the Old Parliament Building, headquarters for UNCHE. Kids in patched, faded denims, carrying backpacks and sleeping bags, arrived daily by thumb or train, looking mostly a little lost, like farm boys in Gotham. This was the "army" of rebellious youth Stockholm had feared being overrun by, who actually turned up in small, very peaceful, sometimes bewildered numbers. Some of the kids came expecting (this being the Sweden of free love, art films, and benign socialism) to sleep free in the parks. But sleeping is prohibited in Stockholm's parks. One afternoon I'd been listening to a program of speeches

and music put on by Alternative City in the Kungsträdgård. As I was leaving, I recognized Dai Dong conferee
Satish Kumar and his wife stretched out head to head on a
long park bench. Behind them, a fountain's spray shim-
mered in the warm afternoon sunlight. I was about to go
over to say hello when I noticed they were sleeping. The
park was full of people, some strolling, others at tables of
the outdoor cafes or sitting quietly on the benches, reading
or chatting. In the background I could still hear thinly the
sounds of the amplified speechmakers and folk singers. It
was a charming vignette—the brown-skinned Indian in his
long muslin tunic, asleep with his pale British wife, utterly
at peace among peaceful strangers. This is what it's all
about, thought I, and felt a thrill of hope for the world.
Next day, I mentioned to Satish that I'd seen him sleeping
in the park, but hadn't wanted to disturb him. No more than
a minute or two after I'd gone, he told me, a policeman had
brusquely wakened them to inform them they were breaking the law, and could be fined for lying down and closing
their eyes. Poof!

But all those kids were going to have to sleep somewhere. It was certainly better to find them a place than to
have them on the streets and in the parks, and have to go
around arresting them. So the city agreed to designate
Skarpnäck, an abandoned military airfield on the outskirts
of town, as the official UNCHE campground, and to set up
virtually a small city of old Swedish army tents, complete
with medical tent for cuts, bruises, and crashing. Stewart
Brand, genius of *The Whole Earth Catalog*, had brought
the Hog Farm over to Stockholm. Hog Farm is an American
commune that lives in a caravan of old buses. They came,
buses and all, to organize free living and free food at
Skarpnäck—a skill they have developed by feeding the
freaky crowds at gatherings like Woodstock. They came also
just to keep things cool. One of the Hog Farmers described
what they do as "a sort of show, but with no distinction
between life and the show." They were good. They had an
efficient mess operation going, serving stuff like brown rice
and beans, mostly, and anyone who wanted to could eat

free. If you ate, they asked you to wash your fork and spoon and plate in the basins set up at the end of the mess line. It wasn't the smörgåsbord they served downtown at the Grand Hotel, but it didn't cost, and it was regular. And things stayed cool.

The city had wanted to charge a camping fee of ten crowns a head at Skarpnäck. They had to charge the fee, they explained, because that was the regular charge at all public campgrounds. If they waived the fee this time, everybody would want to camp for nothing. Domino theory. The Hog Farm flatly refused to go along. It's got to be free, man. That's the whole point of the thing, they told the bureaucrats. The Swedes gave in, muttering, and Skarpnäck was free (except for several incongruously capitalist but thriving hot-dog stands).

The Hog Farm ran a bunch of public programs on a temporary stage they built: a "Rainbow Population Night," featuring talk with the controversial author of *The Population Bomb*, Paul Ehrlich; another evening of talk with Margaret Mead; a "Celebration of Life"; a "Whale Day," for which they had dressed one of their buses in gray plastic to resemble a whale (which it didn't). Always a good feeling out there—lots of grass and music and dancing and people just milling contentedly around, talking, looking. But the programs themselves weren't exciting. Speakers saved themselves for other, more official affairs, and the events were just too unorganized (spontaneous, to be charitable) to amount to much. Hog Farmers played vaguely hypnotic, interminable music on the stage—amplified rock guitars, rock drums with the bottoms exploded out like the bells of horns, electric organ, and a miscellaneous sprinkling of country fiddle, banjo, and mouth harp players— while others milled or danced in a desultory way. The feeling was good, but it wasn't in their planned things that any serious ideas were put forth; it was in the way of life of the Farmers and those who joined them. The openness, the simple pleasure-taking, the freedom to act crazy must have been a source of wonder to the orderly Swedes—to the orderly rest of us, for that matter. Maurice Strong got

out to Skarpnäck for Whale Night; he felt more at home
with the Farm, he said, than he did at the U.N. They
handed him a plate of beans, and he dug right in. Before
he could swallow a reporter asked him what he was doing
here.

"What am I doing here?" Strong mumbled incredu-
lously through his beans. "I'm eating beans. What does it
look like I'm doing?" The reporter asked if the beans were
good; Strong said they were.

It may well be that the whole thing in Stockholm, Dai
Dong, UNCHE, Hog Farm, and all, was only a benevolent
entertainment, with a very great distinction between life
and the show. Chief Hog Farmer Wavy Gravy, who went
around in jester's denim motley, complete with scarlet cap
and bells, certainly didn't add to the sense of reality, which
seemed to recede as the euphoric June weeks went by. But
whatever was going on in Stockholm, the Hog Farm's camp
at Skarpnäck was as real a part of it as Strong himself, or
Lady Jackson, or the Russians (who weren't there), or
Shirley Temple (who was).

But if even the straightest city bureaucrats ended up
grudgingly pleased with Hog Farm's performance, other
Swedes weren't. The Farmers' indulgence in the pleasures
of dope led to a surprisingly bitter attack on them, not by
up-tight city fathers or cops, but by an odd coalition of
equally dour Swedish abstinence freaks and radical Marx-
ists. The clash came at a program sponsored by the People's
Forum, an ad hoc coalition of leftist groups in Scandinavia,
entitled "The Destructive Role of Hog Farm"—the destructive role being that they share their pot like their food with
just about anyone who comes down the pike. Marxist theory, the rads lectured sternly, has always been against anything—religion, drugs, or alcohol—that dulls political consciousness. By using and spreading drugs, they charged, the
Hog Farm was unwittingly collaborating with the capitalist-
imperialist conspiracy to undermine and subvert revolutionary movements. It was a rather typical instance of the
splintering of the political left by nit-picking (in this case
puritan) sectarians. But the Hog Farmers' knack for keep-

ing other people cool is based on their ability to stay cool themselves. They explained patiently to the gray moralists that there are lots of different people in the world, doing a whole lot of different trips, that we all need each other, and that we need to find ways of accepting each other. What kind of drugs are you talking about, one Farmer wanted to know. "Do you mean heroin, cannabis, alcohol, coffee, aspirin . . . ? Personally, I think hard drugs are bad. But I'm for grass—it's good for me." The meeting had a chairman, and there were votes taken, and procedural questions debated, and an agenda. "We're not used to this parliamentary way of doing things," another Farmer remarked afterwards. "We are a family. We sit down and talk things out."

I made a point of going out to Skarpnäck for Rainbow Population Night because clean-cut Stanford Professor Paul Ehrlich was going to speak there, and fireworks had been going off around Paul Ehrlich all day. His name was anathema to the radicals—spat out, not pronounced. Ehrlich's sin is that he advocates public measures of population control to stabilize runaway population growth. It sounds innocent enough on the face of it, even enlightened. But the concept had become explosively politicized, particularly for young third-world radicals who fear it (with considerable justification) as yet another mask for imperialism and genocide. Population had turned unexpectedly into the hottest issue in town. I thought the freaks were really going to let Ehrlich have it. He was plainly tired when he arrived at Skarpnäck, and he sank onto a stool and asked for questions from the audience without giving a speech himself. Kids were sitting around on the grass, huddled in blankets and sleeping bags (for the evenings are always cool in Sweden), couples making love, others smoking, or listening to Ehrlich, or drinking beer and laughing. A hip Swede perched on another stool translated loosely for anyone who cared to hear the remarks in Swedish; mostly he forgot half of what Ehrlich had said. No one minded. No one gave Ehrlich a hard time, either. People were pretty happy. The Hopis from Black Mesa Defense were there. So were assorted curious motorcycle hoods. From across the airfield the sodium lights lining the highway gave their peculiar yellowish cast to the midsummer twilight. Homey columns of smoke rose from the tents into the windless air, the smell of the smoke mixing with the smell of damp grass. Occasionally, someone would race a motorcycle up one of the old runways, then back again; from the highway, traffic noises drifted over in waves. Not much political consciousness here, to be sure, but a tiny capsule of real peace.

All the fancy experts—scientists and economists and savvy politicians—were not more impressive with their expertise than the very simple people, also experts in certain things, who came to Stockholm to keep the experts honest. The victims of mercury poisoning in Minamata Bay, whose twisted, living bodies were their report on pollution. The American Indians who came to appeal to the world to save their lands from the rape of strip-mining. The Indians had been sponsored by Jack Loeffler's Black Mesa Defense Fund and the Sierra Club. There were representatives of ten Indian nations, but the focus of their presence was the destruction of the Hopi's sacred Black Mesa by the Peabody Coal Company, which is stripping the mountain and surrounding land of the coal that lies just under the surface. The coal feeds the giant Four Corners and Mojave power plants, which pollute the Southwestern air to send electrical power to light the garish nights of Las Vegas and L. A. Here, writ small and poignantly, is the whole agonizing conflict between the human being's need for traditional values and a life in balance with the cycles of nature, and his drive for industrial power, for riches, for power to bend the processes of nature to his will.

The Hopis have lived for thousands of years around Black Mesa as sheepherders and farmers, without the benefits of modern, industrial American society. They live today as they have always lived. They do not want the electricity that Las Vegas needs for its dream world of neon light and feathered girls and easy money. The usefulness of Black Mesa to the Hopis is that the mountain is sacred to them, the spiritual center of their religious life. True, the tribal council leased the land willingly and for a price to

Peabody Coal Company, but opponents to the council's action claim that the agreement was a deception: that Peabody did not reveal the extent of their planned excavation, that they paid too little for the lease, that the lease agreement does not provide sufficiently for rehabilitation of stripped land, that Peabody has not provided jobs for Indians (as it promised to do), that the lease is downright illegal. They are fighting now for revocation of the lease. But whatever the legalities of the case, it dramatizes the terrible clash of human interests at the heart of the environmental crisis.

It is no use seeing in this conflict a struggle between good and evil, or cheering the good guys against the bad. If the Hopis were to win this particular battle, one *would* cheer, of course. But the enemy in the war is a far more complex enemy than the Peabody Coal Company. Jack Loeffler produced a slide show to illustrate the plight of the Hopis at Black Mesa, a slick, multiscreen affair with prerecorded soundtrack. Very expensive. The photographs were beautiful, the editing and continuity flawless—a joy to watch. And since I knew it had been produced for Black Mesa Defense, and since, moreover, I was sitting in the "Willow Gallery," which had been given over to the Indians for their stay in Stockholm, I knew I was supposed to root for the Indians. And I did. The trouble was, everything was beautiful. Even the strip mining. Even the dramatic shots of huge earth-moving machinery raping the land. Even the red, Southwestern sun going down behind man-made mountains of coal. Very impressive, with truly poignant juxtapositions of sad, weathered Hopi faces on multiple screens, and all. But if I hadn't known, or been told, the show wouldn't have demonstrated to me that the Peabody Coal Company was exploiting the Hopis and their land. Everything looked so good. Dub in a new soundtrack, and Peabody itself could use the show to advertise how they are bringing the benefits of development to the Indians, for whom they have a really terrific amount of concern.

The problem with the slide show was a confusion of aims. The propaganda got too prettied up in the desire to dazzle. But the show's visual ambiguity illustrates unintentionally the deep ambiguity at the heart of the environmental problem. If there are people who worship the Earth Mother at Black Mesa, who don't want electricity and the degrading of nature it drags along with it, there are other people—lots of them—who really want what Peabody Coal Company can give them—not only want, but clamor for Caesar's Palace and The Sands and the wilderness of Hollywood. And if it stands in the way, one more mountain in a desert not on the triple-A scenic route is nothing to them. Even the Hopis were ready to compromise *some* of their sacred land for the promise of money and jobs. And who blames them? Human values conflict.

The Indians were an incongruous and beautiful presence in Stockholm. They were almost everywhere, dressed as though they were home, the men in denims, faded and worn from honest work, or colorful checked shirts and Western-style pants, with headbands and beads and silver buckles, the women in native dresses, with silver and turquoise jewelry. They told their message simply, in understatement that stood out sharply from the noisy rhetoric of others. One night during the week before UNCHE, I went to a party for the Indians at the Willow Gallery in downtown Stockholm. The basement gallery was jammed. Against one wall, some kids played country music—fiddle, banjo, a tambourine, maybe some improvised pounding and jingling instruments I couldn't see through the crowd. Others were dancing around them, rather exhibitionistically, I couldn't help feeling, though veiled in the aspect of freedom and joy. Occasionally the random dancing of the group would coalesce into the parody of an Indian dance, with a lot of bobbing of heads and whooping which the kids meant as an expression of solidarity with all oppressed native peoples. The Indians, scattered about the crowd, talking quietly mostly among themselves, and drinking, didn't seem to notice. Probably it wouldn't have occurred to an Indian that all that whooping and carrying on was supposed to resemble his own rituals. Just a bunch of crazy kids. I recognized some people from Hog Farm, a woman

in a flour-sack dress, a man with a striped blanket slung
Mexican-style over one shoulder, the man with the blond
horsetail who'd asked about the inner environment. While
I was squeezing through the crowd toward the bar, I came
face to face with a tough-looking Indian in faded denim
pants and jacket. He looked me in the eye and said, "I'm
Coyote. Who are you?" It rattled me. He kept looking at
me with just the hint of a smile on his face so I couldn't tell
if he was being friendly or threatening. Was his name really
Coyote, or was he having a little fun with his Indian cronies
at the paleface's expense? I mumbled my name at him, and he
kept looking at me, waiting for me to account for myself,
I felt. I couldn't account for myself nearly as satisfactorily
as he had, so I nodded inanely, and pushed on to the bar.
In the exact middle of the room, pasha-like, sat Margaret
Mead in her cape, her black, forked walking stick held in
her lap. She was surrounded by a circle of cross-legged lis-
teners, their heads tilted back. I couldn't hear what she was
saying; I could only see the tiny pointed tip of her tongue
dart, now and then, from between her lips, as though punc-
tuating phrases. It was altogether a loud, silly party, which
the Indians endured stoically—which they genuinely enjoyed,
perhaps. They were smiling, anyhow.

The next evening, Dai Dong presented a panel discussion at the ABF House with Al Hassler, two of the conference participants, Margaret Mead, and several of the
Indians from Black Mesa Defense. It wasn't a highly organized program. A few people had just been asked to talk
informally on whatever aspect of the environmental issue
they wished. The idea was to give the public some notion of
Dai Dong's philosophy, and of what the organization was
up to in Stockholm. Margaret Mead—who had been invited
to participate in the Independent Conference, but who
agreed only to be loosely affiliated with it—was something
of a ringer on the program. The panelists didn't get
together beforehand to work out or integrate their topics,
and they simply spoke in the order in which they happened
to sit behind the long table on stage. The group had a nice
balance, appropriate to Dai Dong's vision of a world com-

munity: a Marxist sociologist from Yugoslavia, a Buddhist monk from Vietnam, an anthropologist from the United States, a group of native Americans (i.e., Indians), and the American executive director of Dai Dong. There was more than a fitting balance of human types and persuasions, however; the program took on an unexpected, certainly an unplanned coherence around the theme of alienation and the desperate need to tear down the walls that separate people from each other.

Rudi Supek of Yugoslavia began the evening, speaking in round, capacious, Slavic English. He spoke of human history up to the present moment as a particular phase, a phase of accumulation of political and technological power. By and large, he said, rationality, on the basis of which man prides himself as being uniquely distinct from other animals, has been employed in the accumulation of this power. At the present time, however, we can see that this phase of history is at a point of crisis because the pursuit of power, rational within its own terms, has been *irrational* with respect to humanity—humanity considered not only in the present, but as a continuing species. Man has indeed amassed the power he has sought, but at the expense both of the environment on which his continued existence depends and of the large majority of humanity which has been exploited in the pursuit of power by the few. Worse, the technocratic structure on which power has come more and more to rest has an increasingly dehumanizing effect on the species itself. Supek called for a new vision of man, and for the building of a movement to build a sense of global community, to struggle against the dehumanization of technocracy, and to bring the world successfully through the present crisis into a new, progressive phase of history.

Next, Thomas Benyaka, a round-face Hopi from Black Mesa, spoke briefly. He had come to Stockholm, he said, "to be part of this movement reaching out for the unity of mankind." This unity is the philosophy and goal of the Hopi nation. "*Hopi* means *peace*," he said. "Any nation, any race, anywhere, able to learn to live among themselves in a peaceful way, with nature, could be called *Hopi*." Benyaka introduced David, a religious initiate of the Hopis, his thin face leathery and wrinkled from eighty years or more in the Southwestern sun. Together, the two Indians chanted a prayer—a prayer for those in the audience, and for all living things. Benyaka, who beat out the rhythm on a large drum, explained that the chant was an appeal to the natural elements, to the Great Spirit, the rain gods, the winds and sun and sky and earth. Later in the evening, a striking young Navajo woman, splendidly dressed in deerskin boots and a wine-red dress, with silver buckles and bracelets, sang a traditional song in her own language. "It's about walking in beauty and happiness," she said.

Thich Nhat Hanh, dressed in the brown robes of the contemplative, his dark, ascetic eyes like deep wells, also spoke of phases of history. There is a community of man, he said, but a deeply divided community, "a community in which members do not understand each other, a community in which members continue to exploit each other." He spoke quietly, pausing after each sentence to form the next as though his words were colored stones, each thought part of a mosaic laid out in his mind, then carefully transferred to a wall, stone by stone, for everyone to see. There are two great phases of history. At first, man is threatened by nature, seeks to protect himself and then to master nature, to conquer it. When he has conquered nature, he exploits it for his own ends. "But as soon as he has enough from nature," he said, "he turns against his fellow man and he exploits man. And we are in that second phase of man's history." Man's exploitation of his fellow, however, is the result of a failure of communication—not only among men, but within the individual himself. The development of global communications media has given us the impression that we understand a great deal about the world. "But in fact we understand very little. . . . I speak some English, but that does not mean I can express myself well and that you can understand me. I feel very alone." Just as this inner gulf is fixed between thoughts and words, those who have seen death in Vietnam only on their televisions do not know the reality of it. "If you have been under the bombs,

if you have held in your hands the corpse of a baby, and if
you have tried to bury the rotten corpse, you know that the
images you saw on the television screen are not the reality."
But the dying in Vietnam, the war that tears the people
limb from limb, does not go on because the Vietnamese
people love to kill each other. War becomes necessary
because of the way we have structured our world community. Thus, it is not a Vietnamese conflict, but a world conflict, that rages there. The weapons of war do not go on
being produced because the continuation of war makes
them necessary. Rather, war is made necessary because the
structure of society is built upon the fabrication of weapons.

In Peru, Nhat Hanh went on, most of the people suffer
from a lack of protein. There are tremendous amounts of
protein in the anchovies that supply the Peruvian fishing
industry. But only 5 to 10 percent of the catch is eaten by
the people of Peru. The other 90 percent goes into poultry
and cattle feed in the United States, France, and Great
Britain, because those countries have invested their capital
in the Peruvian fishing industry. "So in the piece of beef-
steak, there is life of the people who are deprived of life.
. . . There are so many simple things that we cannot see,
cannot feel, just because we are unable to communicate."
It is not the unequal distribution of resources that is the
real source of human misery in the world. It is that man
does not know man, but lives isolated in the shell of his
daily life. "*Dai Dong*," he explained, "means . . . the world
of the great togetherness; as I saw it in an ancient Chinese
book, it means a world where people consider everyone's
children as theirs, and everyone's family as theirs."

But the juncture of history at which we find ourselves is
critically dangerous. I am not optimistic that man can survive it, he said, because it requires him to move into a new,
third phase of history, and people are too taken up with
their everyday lives, too hopelessly locked into their shells,
to find the new way. The new way must begin with a turning inward to struggle against two great enemies within
man, his inability to understand his fellow man and his
overriding need to consume. Our social system is the direct

result of our pattern of consumption. The third phase of history, "the Dai Dong world," can only come about through a revolution, he said, "a revolution not outside of man, but a revolution inside of man."

Margaret Mead, who followed, saw the impetus for the needed revolution coming from the environmental crisis itself. She spoke, she said, as an anthropologist, and from that viewpoint she enlarged on Nhat Hanh's theme of isolation. "I have lived with people who included only five or six hundred people among their definition of true and real humanity, and excluded the rest of the world from being as human as themselves." Man, she went on, has one critical characteristic that other living things either do not have at all, or have in only slight degree. Man is able to think of, to comprehend, that which is distant, "distant in the past, distant in the future, and distant in space." This imaginative capacity allows man to conceive of ancestors and future generations, even though he never sees them, and the same capacity allows him to invent the political concept of the nation. It is a connectedness between what is present and what is distant, but (as Nhat Hanh had illustrated with his example of war on the television screen) it is only a partial connectedness—an ambivalent one, at any rate. For it is this ability that makes war possible. Man is able to war against a distant enemy "because he can turn those whom he thinks of either into other human beings like himself, whom he identifies as members of the same human community, or into non-human beings whom he can think of as he thinks of animals that he might kill for meat, or as those who might kill *him* as if *he* were an animal. . . . He learns to think of many other human beings as either prey or predator. This is a peculiarly human capacity." Paradoxically, though, the same imaginative capacity that makes war possible also makes possible the religious concept of the brotherhood of man, and as we have enlarged our technical capacity to make war against ever-larger numbers of people, we have enlarged as well our capacity to conceive of those numbers as truly a human community.

But how are we to transcend the destructive side of this

human capacity to imagine people we cannot see? "As we've looked at . . . the last twenty-five years, as all the people on this planet have come into reach of each other, as we know who's here, and where they are, and that they're all one human species, and as we've come to know how much we're all endangered . . . we've wondered what was going to give us a new way in which we could put things together." After Hiroshima it was thought by many that the threat of nuclear war would finally bring men together in the recognition of the suicidal senselessness of further war. But nuclear weapons became instead simply a new vehicle for conventional, saber-rattling belligerence. When the leaders of government discovered that they could not possibly use nuclear bombs by dropping them on people, they stockpiled them instead to use as blackmail. "But the knowledge that we could endanger this entire planet, the knowledge that we could destroy the atmosphere that stood between us and the sun, the knowledge that we could destroy the oceans that cooled this planet is very new. We had poetic visions, we had religious visions, but we didn't have the scientific underpinnings of that position." Environmental collapse is the first true apocalypse, for the global crisis we now face cannot, like nuclear weapons, be channeled into chauvinistic or ideological warfare. There is no way in the face of the environmental crisis except to come together to save the earth for all of us. The environmental crisis, which is the greatest danger to life on the planet, turns out to be also its greatest opportunity for a salvation it has sought for centuries.

Margaret Mead leaned back in her chair, holding her forked walking stick crosswise over her breast. It was the Indians' turn to speak again. This time it was unexpectedly an ambush, by Gerald Wilson, the well-fed young Hopi who was acting as spokesman for the group of Indians that evening. He talked like an aspiring politician. Loads of drama. And he made a point of quoting Kahlil Gibran. Margaret Mead had inadvertently touched a sore spot when she referred to Indians as "the first settlers of America."

"I didn't come here to start a war," Wilson began por-

tentously, "but I don't think that there's a time in history
when there was an anthropologist on one hand and an
Indian on the other hand when there was not something
that may have been communicated and it was perhaps done
a little bit wrong." If Wilson's mouthful of words was vague,
his condescending tone was clearly hostile. The audience
fidgeted. "Always, always, there were two things that came
to Indian territory. One of them was God. Somebody came
with a Bible and told us about God. And he said, to everybody that listened to him, 'It doesn't matter what you do—
it doesn't make a damn bit of difference what you do—as
long as you believe in *God*, then you'll be saved! And you
can do anything that you want to.' And they did it to my
people. And they're doing it all over the world." He sounded
like the fiery Bible-toter himself. "And then came the anthropologist into Indian territory, and the anthropologist
said, 'So we are the second settlers, and they [the Indians,
Wilson meant the anthropologist meant] were the first settlers.' And thereby they [the anthropologists] destroyed
everything that God didn't destroy, because they told everybody that we came from someplace else."

Margaret didn't flinch, and Wilson went on to something else, not pausing to invite a retort. But the Indians had
come to Stockholm with a real message that went beyond
the vacuity of Wilson's rhetoric. Their message really re-
volved, not around a scientific theory of origins, but around
the Indians' sense of spiritual identity with their land. The
earth is our mother, they say. First the white settlers, then
the American government with troops of soldiers have
greedily taken us from our land, separated the children
from their Earth Mother. We have been forced onto the
reservation, or forced to assimilate into middle-class Western society, or simply annihilated outright. The government
has used both Christian mythology and anthropological
theory to justify its crimes of rape and genocide. When the
Indians insist that they were never settlers in America, that
they did not come from anywhere else, that they came from
the earth on which they live, and that they belong to it as

children to their mother, they are making a religious statement, not a scientific one.

Coyote, the tough, laconic Wailaki from California
whom I'd run into at the gallery party, made the point with
an anecdote. He came on stage dressed in his denim work
clothes and thanked everyone for "being host," as he put it
wrily, "to the wild people of America." Coyote was plainly
proud of his wildness, in which, Thoreau has said, is the
preservation of the world. The true wildness of the native
American is not the character of the Hollywood wild
Indian. Coyote had come to tell people that what they had
read in books and seen in movies and on television about
Indians was not true. The wildness of the Indian is simply
his oneness with nature, his mother. "When I was small, I
was educated in a public school, and I read about Vikings—
very fierce people who put fear into the world. And I came
to meet Vikings. And I couldn't find any. I asked the people
—I said, 'Did all the descendants move away?' They said,
'No, but that was a long time ago.'" The Vikings have
disappeared, but time has not changed the character of the
Indian. "David, that prayed for all of you," Coyote went on,
"he is no different from the people that went by a long time
ago. He's still the same man as our ancestors, . . . Through
people like David we still maintain the spirit."

The evening was closed by Al Hassler. "I wanted to say
a little about Dai Dong," he began, "but I hardly know how
to after this program, because people have been talking
about Dai Dong all evening. That's what it is. I can't tell
you it's an organization, because it isn't. We have no members, and yet we represent a community that has millions
of members. We have a staff, but we have no centralized
control. We have a program, but we don't want anybody to
write in and ask to join it.

"Dai Dong is the conception that we have come to a
moment in history that is unprecedented, when we are
literally all in the same boat, when we cannot any longer
war against each other, but must war against those qualities
of the human character that have kept us in subjection to

greed, and that we must do it together. Dai Dong is an attempt to create projects and endeavors that will dramatize this reality and raise the consciousness of people all over the world of the genuinely desperate plight that we are in, because only as we become conscious and spread that consciousness can there possibly be a large enough political force to make the very radical changes in social, political, and economic institutions that are required."

Hassler explained that Dai Dong was a part of the movement to create the sense of world community of which Thich Nhat Hanh had spoken. But his vision was no more filled with blissful optimism than the stoical contemplative's. To create the global community on which our salvation depends is nearly impossible in the face of (as he had put it earlier) "those qualities of the human character that have kept us in subjection to greed." On the contrary, he said, "Only the best impulses of the human spirit can fashion the new community of the world." It was a felicitous phrase to end an evening of talk and prayer and song by a Marxist sociologist and an anthropologist on the one hand, and "the wild people of America" on the other. "The best impulses of the human spirit"—it embraces nicely what each person who spoke or sang offered (except for that momentary, quixotic ambuscade), embraces man's intellect, and his emotions, and his sense of beauty, as it recognizes that in each one of us lie the seeds of our world's end.

III

Two Worlds

The Dai Dong Conference opened on Thursday, the first of June. Sunday the fourth was to be given over to rest and recreation in Stockholm, and the public evening with Margaret Mead and the Indians. That left four solid working days, plus a short morning, in which to complete the declaration, promised for a noon press conference on Tuesday, the sixth. At the opening plenary, Al Hassler expressed the hope that the work groups would finish quickly with the declaration itself, and move on to develop specific proposals for action. The staff's experience at Menton, he explained, had suggested that a group of scientists ought not to try writing a document together, and therefore the staff had prepared the draft declaration, not to preempt what the conference would, in the end, declare, but rather to provide a general framework from which the group could proceed. The declaration was not, after all, going to be a scientific paper. It seems clear even to many laymen what, in general, needs to be said. The task of the conference, Hassler went on, was not to worry over commas, semicolons, and niceties of diction. The staff, principally Dorothy Maas, the witty and luckily patient assistant director of Dai Dong, would serve as editorial committee. The idea was for the conference quickly to identify areas of agreement with the draft, correct points of disagreement, and fill in any omissions. Then the conference would be free to get on with the second task, that of formulating concrete recommendations.

Almost everyone agreed on the need for recommendations. Fred Knelman reported to the plenary the reaction of the work group on security and war to the prepared draft. "One major point the whole group agreed upon is that this document will be strengthened immeasurably if we append to it or include within it some specific and seemingly (at least) realizable recommendations—that as it stands it is a fine statement, it is beautiful and profound, but it does lack specificity." As it turned out, the conference only barely completed its first task, the declaration. Hannes de Graaf, the fatherly dean of the University of Utrecht, and forbearing chairman of this sometimes tumultuous conference, expressed skepticism early on about the chances for reaching a consensus on recommendations in only four or five days. But it never even came to a question of consensus on recommendations; consensus on what to declare proved hard enough to coax out of the gathering.

In the same work group's report to the plenary, Knelman less charitably summed up reaction to the draft: "The general feeling of our group was that the whole declaration lacked a kind of sharpness, strength. It was generally, not exactly clichéd, but written in a pious, generalized way, and we felt that the entire document required sharpening." The document required not only sharpening, however. There were, as it turned out, three areas of profound disagreement among conference participants. The staff knew ahead of time that these would be the sensitive areas, but it was quite unprepared for the depth of the division over them, which threatened at several points to tear the conference apart, or at least to result in the omission of statements crucial to the declaration.

The first serious bone of contention was the draft's unequivocal condemnation of the principle of national sovereignty. It was mostly third-world people who remained adamant that the newly acquired sovereignty of their nations was their only hedge against the aggrandizement of the rich and powerful. Second, the question of support for wars of liberation split the conference sharply between those who were categorically opposed to war and those who saw

war as necessary, as a last recourse, to throw off oppression.
Third, and most explosive, most divisive of all, was the
question of population: on one side were those who saw
some form of population control as an indispensable part
of any long-range strategy to protect the environment; on
the other were those, mostly third-world people, who saw
concealed behind *any* form of population control a policy of
neoimperialist oppression and genocide. These difficulties
kept the conference wrangling over the wording of the declaration right through the morning of the press conference
at which the declaration was to be publicly presented. The
declaration that finally was read to the press just after lunch
on Tuesday was thus a thoroughly rewritten document, and
this rewriting took up all the time and energy of the conference, and would have taken more had there been any. For
the differences were not primarily scientific, but political, and
politics is a maw insatiable for controversy.

On the first day, with long days of group and plenary
meetings stretched out like a vista ahead, when the thirty-
odd scientists from two dozen countries (many struggling
with English) were still feeling each other out on style and
ideology, there was some general discussion in the work
groups, and some specific proposals for action not directly
related to the declaration itself. The idea of redistribution of
resources and technology, for instance, came up early and
repeatedly in most of the groups. However it might be real-
ized, everyone saw the urgent need for some form of equalization of wealth throughout the world. As it is, the enormous disparity between rich and poor, both within nations
and internationally, is at the heart of the hopelessly vicious
cycle of poverty whereby the rich get richer and the poor
get poorer. Development, after all, is a relative thing. There
is no absolute state of "development" that the industrialized
nations have reached, and the "developing" nations are
aiming at. In fact, the very terms "developed" and "developing" are misleading because they suggest a static rather
than a dynamic model of the world, according to which the
"developing" nations will sooner or later wind up where the
"developed" nations are now, and then things will be all

squared up. Actually, the "developing" nations could not
wind up where the "developed" are now even if they wanted
to (which they do—many of them—third-world rhetoric not-
withstanding). Even if they could, the "developed" nations
would by that time have proceeded on their own way to somewhere else, stretching the gap between rich and poor—
already a yawning gulf—wider than ever.

To begin with, the conditions in most "developing"
countries are utterly unlike the conditions in the "developed." The industrialized nations are almost all in temperate
climates, for example, while the nonindustrialized nations
are mostly in desert, tropical, or subtropical regions. Many
of these countries are attempting to move directly from
tribal or feudal social systems into industrialization, and
most depend on technical and managerial assistance from
the outside. Where conditions differ radically, we can't look
for similar results. Second, it is not likely that the historical
evolution of the presently industrialized nations will repeat
itself, just as biological evolution does not repeat itself, but
creates ever new, unimaginable forms. It is impossible to
imagine the forms mutation will create in nature; it may be
equally impossible to imagine with precision the forms our
future social, economic, and political development will take.
We can only guess that they will be as radically different
from present forms as mammals are from reptiles. In the
meantime, the attempt to emulate "development" in the
nonindustrialized countries threatens to result not in the
image of industrialization, but in a parody of it—the urban
sprawls of Africa and Asia, for instance, in contrast to
which Detroit or Hoboken seem pleasant, or glossy come-
ons for soft drinks and fast cars directed incongruously at
people who are chronically hungry, who are retarded and
diseased through malnutrition, who are not expected to live
beyond a wretched, thirty-fifth year. This phase of parody,
which we see in many third-world countries, is itself one of
the conditions that differ so radically from those that determined the development of industrialized nations, and it will
serve as a powerful determinant in the historical progress
of the presently "developing" nations toward their own,

heretofore unimaginable social, economic, political, and industrial forms.

Certainly if some substantial and more equitable distribution of wealth in the world does come about, our own future in the industrialized countries will be very different from a projection based on the assumption of continued economic growth in the currently accepted sense. For the growth on which present economic stability rests is in turn dependent on the present global system, and thus dependent on inequality and exploitation; to right inequality and exploitation means nothing less than radically changing, revolutionizing, the present industrial system.

The question of redistribution arose in one work group in response to a dramatic admonition from Yusuf Eraj, a gynecologist and family-planning expert from Kenya. He asked members of his group, who had been discussing how to mobilize public opinion on environmental matters, to remember that the great majority of mankind, who live what he called a subhuman existence of malnutrition and hunger, cannot concern themselves with any but their own immediate problems of staying alive today, perhaps tomorrow. "If we lock a man in a room and don't give him any food," he said, "he will die in about six days. But if we give him half the food he needs, it will take him twenty years to die. The average span of life in the developing countries at the moment is between thirty and thirty-five years. These people are not living; they are dying a slow death all the time." Theoretically at least, the cure to malnutrition and starvation on a global scale is a matter of redistribution, since we know that the industrialized countries could today produce the minimum protein and vitamin requirements for the whole world's population. Bengt Hubendick of Sweden asked cautiously whether, if food could be equally distributed throughout the world, population would not simply explode, replacing one disastrous problem with another. Eraj replied heatedly that this was wishful thinking: "The question is entirely hypothetical. It has no reality." The question is unreal, we might add, in exactly the way projections based on the static notion of "developed" and "developing" countries are unreal. It is as pointless to speculate on hypothetical cases of zero probability as to dispute a pinhead's capacity for angels.

University of Rochester biologist Conrad Istock pointed out that equitable distribution of resources and technology over the globe—however it is achieved—would be much less polluting than the present disposition, since spreading out the sources of pollution would avoid the poisonous concentrations that plague the industrialized world today and would give the ecosphere a chance to absorb and recycle the materials discharged into it. Many of the conference participants believed that a just redistribution of wealth is not possible so long as the industrialized world is committed to growth as it is now understood; they saw the necessity for those economies to alter their goal from growth to the achievement of equilibrium, of "steady-state." Economist Nicholas Georgescu-Roegen countered that the ideal of steady-state is not enough. We cannot have a system that produces goods on the basis of fashion and obsolescence, even if it maintains a state of equilibrium, he said. We must instead transform the values that govern the economy. Growth is not evil in itself, he argued; the problem is that growth has become a self-justifying ideology. We need instead to make constantly the rational determination: growth for what? In the present crisis our priority ought to be to devote resources and energy toward the reduction of pollution rather than toward economic growth. Georgescu-Roegen was uneasy about the concept of redistribution, since, stated thus, it fails to take into account individual and regional needs and possibilities. This was also the concern of third-world people in Stockholm, who feared the zero-growth ideology as another guise of imperialist oppression.

Ernst Winter, who also served as consultant to the UNCHE Secretariat, objected for another reason to the term redistribution. "I can hear that," he said, "I heard it, exactly like that at the prep com [preparatory committee for UNCHE]. Anybody can say that, and those who are in the establishment will say it, you see, and nothing will change. So what is it uniquely we are adding that will make

a difference? Because you know the redistribution of resources—everybody's in favor of that. I can give you an
argument of McNamara's, who said redistribution is exactly
what the World Bank is here for. But the one thing the
World Bank is *not* doing when it approves a project . . .
Maurice Strong had a long lunch with McNamara, and
when he suggested that a project must also be considered on
the basis of environmental criteria, McNamara said, that's
none of our business. The World Bank is here to redistribute
resources."[1] Mindless redistribution is as bad as or worse than
none at all, Winter was arguing. "Electrical power is being
redistributed," he went on. "They're building more and
more lines all over the landscape—you can hardly see the
sky. And the UNDP [United Nations Development Pro-
gramme] is lending money for it. So what is really missing
here? I think what is missing is that we must involve in the
redistribution process people who have been excluded from
it. Distribution has always been governed by some elite.
The *people* ought to be redistributing things." Involving people in this process is an opening wedge in the struggle to
transcend the present governmental structure of power.
"This environmental crisis must be used to bring people
into the game. And not through representative bodies, and
not through political parties, and not through governments,
but *people—people* must participate. We're not just asking
for redistribution. We're asking for nongovernmental, non-
elitist, nonestablishment control by the people themselves
of the things that concern them."

Two concrete proposals for redistribution emerged
from the work groups. Most dramatic was Georgescu-
Roegen's idea that the Dai Dong Conference affirm the

[1] Winter's information was perhaps out of date; in any case, it was
apparently contradicted by McNamara in his address to the plenary
session of UNCHE. "Each project processed in the Bank is now re-
viewed by the Environmental Office, and a careful in-house study is
made of the ecological components. . . . While in principle the Bank
could refuse a loan on environmental grounds . . . the fact is that no
such case has yet arisen. Since initiating our environmental review, we
have found that in every instance the recommended safeguards can
and have been successfully negotiated and implemented." Reprinted
in *Science and Public Affairs*, Vol. 28, No. 7 (Sept., 1972), pp. 39–43.

right of each human being to freedom of movement across
political borders. The proposal amounts to a redistribution
of resources through redistribution of population. If resources denied to the people of one region are available
somewhere else, they ought to be free to go there. This principle would extend the United Nations Universal Declaration of Human Rights' Article 13, which affirms that "(1)
Everyone has the right to freedom of movement and resi-
dence within the borders of each state. (2) Everyone has
the right to leave any country, including his own, and to
return to his country." The U.N. affirms the right of everyone to leave any country; Georgescu-Roegen would affirm
the right of everyone also to enter any country.

The idea was met with considerable suspicion at first.
Wouldn't the industrialized nations be overrun by the
world's poor? After some discussion, however, Conrad
Istock (at least) expressed enthusiastic support for the proposal. He argued that it might well be the keystone to the
whole issue of development and the distribution of wealth.
If people were free to move to where resources are, then all
governments would be under real pressure to cooperate
toward the end of equitable distribution. The government
that would fail to make its country desirable loses the population on which it depends. In fact, the first to go would
be those it could least afford to lose, professionals and
technicians. The wealthy government that failed to aid
poorer nations, in turn, would face an influx of population
it probably would not be prepared to accommodate, and
would suffer the consequences of overcrowding. Such a government would not long be permitted by its citizens to hold
power. Or so Istock's argument ran.[2]

---

[2] The declaration of any human right as universal is of course utopian, and thus essentially rhetorical. One would have to imagine,
in the case of the right of free movement, that no country could declare itself "full," and stop immigration by force. Istock's argument
appears further to assume that an Afghanistani peasant, say, would
actually be able to move half way across the globe to the U.S., for
example, assuming he heard he had the right to move, and believed
what he heard.

Another proposal for redistribution was Fred Knelman's idea for a world protein bank into which the industrialized nations would deposit surplus protein for distribution among the undernourished nations. As an example he cited the six billion pounds of whey, a by-product of the cheese industry, that is dumped annually into Canadian waters. Whey is rich in protein, and is thus a valuable resource. Dumped in high concentrations as industrial waste into streams and rivers, however, it becomes a major water pollutant. Processing this whey for deposit in a world protein bank would thus have the double effect of saving for those who desperately need it valuable nutrients that would otherwise be wasted, and of cleaning up the waterways of Canada.

Satish Kumar of India attacked the proposal as paternalism. We don't want your whey, he said archly. We want cheese. I suppose he meant *Indian* cheese, and not just a higher grade of Canadian condescension. But Knelman's proposal had been well-intentioned, and he was visibly taken aback. He asked by way of reply how it was possible to redistribute any wealth at all without some measure of what might be construed as paternalism. Kumar's indignation on the one hand and Knelman's bemusement on the other were only the beginning of what proved to be, throughout the Dai Dong Conference as well as UNCHE, a widening gap of mistrust and misunderstanding between third-world people and people from the industrialized world. Essentially the same gap was apparent in Bolivian Jürgen Schütt-Mogro's objection to the protein bank idea. The problem with such an approach to the need for redistribution, he argued, is that it subverts the revolution by diverting attention and energy from the need for basic change in the socioeconomic and political systems that cause hunger and malnutrition.

The same objection came up again over the idea of "soft" technology—that is, technology that minimizes or eliminates environmental degradation. The discussion in the plenary centered around the need to develop new structures of governance for technologies. Iranian M. Taghi Farvar complained that the draft declaration represented, in this regard, "sort of the Band-Aid approach. It's prescribing reformist solutions, for the most part within the existing systems. There are a number of concepts here that almost entirely show a sort of Western bias. . . . I suggest that what is in fact needed to cure these problems is social revolution."

Protest bristled like hackles on a dog's neck. "What is social revolution?" several people challenged in a chorus. The conference had been talking about social revolution all along, so it wasn't the concept they were objecting to now. Taghi had walked into the conference two days late (with no good account of himself, some felt) and started shooting his mouth off about revolution and third-world perspectives and a lot of other things, which was a way of making himself popular with some, and not with others. He had almost been given up, and the staff people, who'd produced the conference on a pretty frayed shoestring to begin with, couldn't help but wonder if they'd get back the money for his fare. But he showed up after all, and made up for the time he'd missed.

Taghi's face looks beaked, like a hawk's. Curly black hair comes almost to his shoulders; from his temples it flows down in thick muttonchops over his cheeks, then across his mouth as a mustache. Black horn-rims goggle his eyes. His articulate English is flawless (if rhetorical), and though he speaks with a peculiar, clipped intonation hard to place, you wouldn't take him for a foreigner. It's incongruous each time he prefaces a remark, as he's given to doing, "In my own country, Iran . . . " New York seems somehow more likely. His viewpoints derive in large measure from Barry Commoner's, whose student Taghi was at the Center for the Biology of Natural Systems at Washington University in St. Louis. Nevertheless, he says he has the third-world perspective, and the fact is that he very quickly assumed leadership of a group of young participants from the third world, several of whom were also members, with Taghi, of the OI Committee International,[3] an association of young radical third-world scientists formed at the Hamilton Youth Conference in 1971.

"There is no use formulating anything about structures if we are not clear about technology," put in Roel van Duyn, wry genius of the Dutch Kabouters ("Elves"), who succeeded the Provos as subverters and unmaskers of the joyless establishment in Holland. "Because technology is structuring structures. For instance, if you build a nuclear power plant in a country you are creating a very centralized structure." To the technocrat's power plant he opposed windmills as an example of decentralized, nonpolluting sources of power for the people. "If we accept soft technology, then it is feasible to look for a decentralized, socialist revolution. And we have to make [the revolution]. I think we have to say that openly."

Taghi responded that "what is lacking in the idea of soft technology is that it is almost totally devoid of political content. There is no doubt that an environmentally compatible technology—call it by whatever name—is more desirable than an environmentally destructive technology. But . . . the reason why technologies as we know them presently are environmentally destructive and socially exploitative is in fact the nature of the social and economic systems that govern their use and creation and operation. And that is what I mean by the need for social revolution. The structures have to change and those are social and economic, not technological."

"I would like to answer that," van Duyn countered. "Western technology, the hard, poisoning technology, is a technology which is creating centralization and specialization and stabilization of the status quo. . . . If we have a soft technology, we can move the social structures. But if we have hard technology, we cannot move, we are imprisoned. There is a very clear connection between technology and

[3] "OI" is an acronym for a Swahili phrase, "Ote Iwapo," which means "all that is must be considered."

social structure, and I am, for political as much as for environmental reasons, in favor of this soft technology, because it brings to the people the power to use their own devices to fulfill their needs. The decentralization of this soft technology is as important for these reasons as for the sake of the environment."

Somewhere between van Duyn's position, that technology determines structure, and Taghi's, that structures determine technology, was Fred Knelman's position that structure and technology both have to be changed. He rejected the argument of the pessimistic technological determinists that technology inevitably becomes self-perpetuating and self-justifying—that means inevitably subvert ends. "I believe it's still possible through human will and human intervention to redesign society, to *invent* a new society for which there is no precedent, no existing model, in which we still have some kind of science and technology, obviously, but in which there are safeguards, so that there is no ecological backlash, and there is no social backlash. . . . We don't introduce an SST, make it operational, and *then* discover afterwards what all the social costs are. We do all our work in advance. What is the full impact of the SST going to be, environmentally, economically, socially, politically? Or of central data banks, which have a terrible capacity to invade privacy? And we then build into a technology both the ecological safeguards and the social safeguards, the safeguards against social abuse, so that a technology can only be used in an ecologically sound way, and can only be used in a socially constructive way. And this would be true of the new biology, which is perhaps more threatening than anything in its power to manipulate. Within the system as it now exists there is no way of bringing technology under rational control. That's impossible. So what we're talking about in one way or another is a social revolution."

Some of the older people were getting edgy at all this talk of revolution. "Sir," injected P. J. Deoras, physician and entomologist from Bombay, "we are going in rather a tangential way. . . . Revolutions, social and otherwise, have been mentioned here and there, but we can't bring in those words in a declaration which is being presented to the United Nations."

Professor M. A. Chaudhri of neighboring Pakistan respectfully demurred; the old structures have to be replaced, he insisted. "We have to think of the future; how are we going to build a future? It is only by changing the existing structures. It is the existing structures that have failed us. Take the case of the U.N. The U.N. has failed us completely. It is almost a useless body. We have to have something new."

Thich Nhat Hanh worried about the idea of revolution for a reason other than the sensibilities of U.N. delegates. "If we express our design only in terms of a revolution of a system," he said, "and neglect that human element that is the beginning of every change, we may miss the most important point." He was making the same point, really, with which Hannes de Graaf had opened the first plenary: it is neither technology nor structure that will save us, but people. We must stop making the fatal error of trusting our destinies to the machines that have gotten us into this nightmare of a sorcerer's apprentice in the first place. De Graaf had remarked that, in "my own country [Holland], in which the report of the Club of Rome is among the bestsellers at the moment, the mainstream of thought is going in a technological, technocratic direction. They have the feeling that they will control the ecological crisis by technological measures. I think the direction of our thought at this conference will be in the opposite direction—that we feel the need for an ethical, ecological control of the blind technology that, connected with power and greed and lust for profit, have caused the world to run wild."

Suspicion—mutual suspicion—between revolutionary young third-world people and the rest of the conference, people from industrialized Western countries as well as older people from the third world, ran as an undercurrent throughout the Dai Dong Conference, and throughout the U.N. Conference too, and surfaced frequently into open, deep division. In the very first day's meeting of the work group on environment and development, for instance, Jaime Hurtubia, ecologist from Chile, also a member of the OI Committee, complained that the group was focusing exclusively on problems of developed nations. The discussion was not sufficiently informed by the third-world perspective to deal in appropriate terms with problems of industrialization and pollution in the third world. The same lopsided view has resulted in the cultural imperialism that imposes the consumption values of the industrialized West onto developing countries, he argued. In another context, Jurgenne Primavera, biologist from the Philippines, stated "for the record" that all these conferences and statements of white men from developed countries say nothing whatsoever to brown and black people in the third world, because they are unable to see the problems through any but their own white eyes.

Yusuf Eraj emphasized another aspect of the problem of third-world perspective with his example of the man left in a locked room to starve. The people who live the subhuman existence of malnutrition and hunger (which is half the people in the world) are incapable of caring about the environment because they need to feed themselves before anything. Eraj made his point in response to a discussion of the deleterious effects of chemical fertilizers and pesticides. People in the third world have no alternative to the use of such chemicals if they can get them, he said, because in spite of long-term effects, they have to solve their immediate and desperate problems in the short term.

But there was no agreement among third-world people on this point. "When my friend Yusuf speaks for the third world," Satish Kumar replied, "and says that 'agricultural pollution has a different connotation to us,' I don't know how many people he is thinking for. Because . . . organic agriculture has proved . . . in experience to be *more* productive than chemical agriculture." He leaned over the table and the words tumbled out of his mouth in a passionate heap. "It is absolutely Western nonsense, propagandistic brainwashing of the third world that chemical fertilizers are their salvation. . . . China can produce much more food with local, organic compost and manure than twenty years of American chemical fertilizers in India."

Polish soil chemist Jerzy Chodan agreed about the relative productivity of organic fertilizer, but pointed out that in many parts of the world only chemical fertilizers can be used, either because industrialization has removed the animal and human sources of manure and compost from the land by mechanizing agriculture and concentrating human population in the cities, or because the needs simply outstrip the supply of organic fertilizer. He added, however, that modern food processing often works against the higher yields of the green revolution by processing out nutritional elements. Our grandfathers, he said, ate a slice of bread and butter. To get the same biological value today, we have to add a slice of cheese.

Georgescu-Roegen sided with the critics of the green revolution. "Even if it *were* more efficient or more productive today to use artificial fertilizers, it is antiecological." The global system has two principal sources of energy, the stock of fossil fuels buried under the surface of the earth, and the flow of light from the sun. The stock of fuels is finite; the flow of solar energy is virtually limitless. It is estimated, for instance, that all the fossil fuels available on earth, taking into account yet-undiscovered reserves, would equal the energy that reaches the earth in only four days of sunlight. The production of chemical fertilizers and the production and operation of agricultural machinery use up this relatively tiny resource reserve while at the same time increasing the biosphere's burden of pollution. Moreover, this system of mechanization replaces the living system of draft animals and organic fertilizer which draws essentially all its energy from the limitless source of solar radiation, and returns its waste to the soil as nutrient. Our efforts ought to be directed toward minimizing our use of our resource stock, and maximizing our use of the flow of solar radiation. When we waste the finite resources entrusted to us (by default, be it said), we do so at the expense of our children and grandchildren. "We must train people to hear the cries of the last men for air, food, and water," Georgescu-Roegen concluded.[4]

Taghi Farvar, holding fast to his position that there is no substitute for social revolution, denied that responsibility to future generations is the first order of priority. (Georgescu-Roegen hadn't said it was.) The green revolution, he went on, benefits primarily the developed countries and their huge complexes of agribusiness, often at the expense of the underdeveloped countries. As an example he cited the Philippines, once an exporter of rice, which now has to import it because of widespread crop failure resulting from epidemics of a fungus to which the new, dwarf strains are not resistant. In Iran, similarly, in 1967 and 1968, he said, the new varieties of wheat were virtually wiped out in many areas by a wheat rust to which traditional varieties had been resistant. Wherever industrialized agriculture has been introduced, he concluded, the rich have gotten richer, while the poor have been crowded into the cities and made destitute.

The third world *must* use the green revolution, Eraj countered, to supply the proteins and vitamins required to produce whole human beings capable, then, of rebelling against the green revolution and devising a better way. Conrad Istock agreed, and added that even Ernest Borlaug, the Nobel Prize-winning "father" of the green revolution, admits that the green revolution only buys the time in which to find a real and lasting solution to the problem of world hunger—perhaps fifteen years. It isn't a long-term solution. He cited West Pakistan and Ceylon (now Srilanka) as instances of the striking success of the green revolution. "West Pakistan has gone in a matter of a few years from being an importer of food to being an exporter of food. They now have food sufficiency. The green revolution can push a country beyond the minimal caloric sufficiency. Ceylon

---

[4] See Nicholas Georgescu-Roegen, "The Entropy Law and the Economic Problem," in *Toward a Steady-State Economy*, ed. Herman Daly (San Francisco, 1973), pp. 37–49. The full exposition of Georgescu-Roegen's view is to be found in his *The Entropy Law and the Economic Process* (Cambridge: Harvard University Press, 1971).

seems to be about to make it. And once they get a yield of grain that's beyond the caloric sufficiency, they can also solve protein deficiencies, because you can use the grain to feed chickens or cattle. Whatever animal will eat grain will make muscle, and if you eat it you get protein. So in those countries that have adopted the green revolution, I think it's likely that they will either achieve food sufficiency in all respects, or get very close to it—something much grander than they've had in a whole century probably. And many of them will actually become strong agricultural states, as West Pakistan seems to be. And that seems to be making indus-trialization possible. . . . We recognize that these nations are going to have to adopt this, but it should only be looked upon as a way of buying some time in order to find forms of agriculture which can be sustained in the long run. Be-cause it's pretty clear that you can't sustain the green revo-lution for a century. You can look upon the green revolution as a way of very quickly plucking most of the wretched nations of the world up to a state where they can begin a process of rational discourse and intercourse with the rest of the world."

IV

Sovereignty, War, Population

The first of the killer issues, national sovereignty, showed its teeth in the opening work-group meetings. Henry Regier remarked the next morning as we were waiting for breakfast that the Dai Dong delegates seemed barely less committed to national sovereignty and parochial interests than the U.N. delegates themselves. This was admittedly a hyperbole, for the argument over sovereignty had a different meaning in the context of the Independent Conference. But the hyperbole did reflect the bafflement of the Dai Dong staff at finding a position they had come to regard akin to motherhood (a position clearly set forth in the Dai Dong program literature) attacked so vehemently by people they took to be their friends. Again, it was largely a third-world issue. I heard it come up first in the work group on environment and development. UNCHE's draft declaration had stated flatly that sovereignty over natural resources is an "inalienable right" of nations. Dai Dong's draft just as flatly denied that sovereignty is an inalienable right of nations, not only because the Dai Dong philosophy holds sovereignty to be an outmoded concept that serves only to encourage war and oppression and exploitation, but also because so many nations throughout history have discovered empirically that sovereignty often proves sadly alienable indeed. The inalienability of a nation's sovereignty has always been proportional either to its power or to its poverty of exploitable resources. But Jaime Hurtubia, after listening

politely to his colleagues from the industrialized West, finally
raised what he seemed to have been stewing over for an hour
or so. Did Dai Dong's denial of a nation's absolute sovereignty over the resources that happened to be found within its
borders mean, for example, that his own country, Chile, could
not nationalize its copper mines? For centuries the people
of Chile have been exploited by imperialistic interests which
have robbed them of their resources. Now, when these resources are finally in the hands to which they belong, when
this wealth offers the people true independence and autonomy, shall they once again relinquish control over them?

Jurgenne Primavera argued for sovereignty as a hedge
against cultural imperialism. "The bind of Dai Dong's being
transnational and transcending nation states is that you can't
ask the developing countries to jump that step. They have to
go through it in a natural process. For example, the average Filipino now has no identity as a Filipino at all. He
uses a foreign language in his schools. Once you capture the
language of a country it's so much easier to capture the
culture, to replace that with something from the outside.
And this is precisely what American business has done. The
Filipino learns U.S. history before he learns Southeast Asian
history. I mean I don't know a thing about Indonesia—it's
right next door. But I know everything about the U.S. So
I'm very strong about sovereignty—genuine sovereignty—
so that we decide how our educational system will be. In a
local language, O.K.? And then we have some kind of a
consciousness and some kind of a pride. In the Philippines
we don't have that. And that makes me sad."

Kenyan Eraj didn't share her view. He defended the
Dai Dong position forcefully. The whole environmental
crisis really revolves around sovereignty, he argued, around
the fundamental "contradiction between ecology and the
national economics." It is precisely because nations and
corporations are able to invoke the principle of sovereignty
in order to act in only their narrow self-interest that the
earth is endangered. "Nationalism as such must be overcome," added Rudi Supek. "Because nationalism is based
essentially on ethnocentrism and Social Darwinism. That is

the real basis: the struggle for biological expansion. And that is the struggle among ethnic groups. . . . The real essence of all nationalistic movements is Social Darwinism, the struggle to expand one group at the expense of other groups."

Knelman cited the ecological principle that intervention in the operation of a system can be successful only at a level of complexity equal to the complexity of the system. Thus, since environmental problems do not correspond with political borders, but are global in scope, they can be managed only globally, above the level of national sovereignty.

Nigerian Dora Obi Chizea retorted with one of the earthy analogies she's given to. "Sovereignty is not generally understood by those of us in the third world in the same way," she barked out in her husky voice. "You take a gentleman who has lived his years, fifty, sixty, seventy years. In his younger days he had all the women he wanted, and he had all the pleasures of life. Now he is tired; women are not much use anymore. And he says to the young man, 'What are you doing with the girls? Don't you know the evil in women?' It's a concept that is difficult for the young man to grasp."

The laughter cooled the heated meeting a degree, and Executive Director Alfred Hassler, only one or two years from retirement, drew another laugh when he responded defensively, "I get the point, but I don't like the analogy."

Regier suggested that the issue be handled by speaking of "relative regional sovereignty, in effect, without mentioning nations and national sovereignty, arguing a basic sovereignty of all people over the world's resources, recognizing that regional sovereignties will exist."

Economist Georgescu-Roegen, a meticulous scientist driven by a passion for logic no less than for justice, fought constantly to remove what he saw as contradictions in the text of the declaration. There is a contradiction, he said, between calling on the one hand for an end to sovereignty, yet calling on the other for sovereignty, regional or otherwise, over resources. There is just as fundamental a contradiction, he went on, between the declaration's call for redistribution and equalization of the world's wealth among its people and the statement (as the reworked draft at that point in the proceedings had it) that benefits accruing to the extraction and manufacture of resources belong by right to the people of the region where the resources are found.

On other questions—population and war, for instance —Jean Mussard held positions close to those of the young third-world radicals. But he was clearly and firmly opposed to their appeal for national sovereignty. He called for a precise formulation in the declaration of Dai Dong's view that political boundaries are, from an environmental point of view, fictional nonsense. It should be made equally clear, however, that the transcendence of the nation state must not be used as a pretext for the big powers to swallow the small. "I want to draw attention to the fact that *sovereignty* is a technical term. It is a concept which was invented by the lawyers of the feudal European lords. And I am convinced—I may be alone in believing it—that this concept is absolutely obsolete and inadequate for future developments. Of course I understand very well what is in the minds of our friends from the developing countries when they insist on this concept. I merely want to show that technically it is completely wrong and misplaced. It is an obsolete, feudal European concept. Therefore, would it not be more appropriate to speak of local autonomy and basic rights than of basic sovereignty and not use obsolete concepts which have a very precise legal meaning—which had some sense in Europe five hundred years ago?"

"In principle I agree with you," replied Hannes de Graaf. "But I have the strong feeling that in the situation in which we live at the moment, even though this concept of sovereignty is obsolete, the only way for some underdeveloped nations, for instance, to nationalize industry is to use the concept of sovereignty. I think there is no way out at the moment. Here I am in favor of a contradiction."

"It is not really a contradiction," Mussard came back. "It's a bad word."

Georgescu-Roegen sided with Mussard. "To my mind, in the concept of Dai Dong sovereignty doesn't have any place. So I should say instead of basic sovereignty, 'a far-reaching principle of human justice.' It's not logical to speak of sovereignty and redistribution of natural resources at the same time. On the basis of sovereignty the states which you want now to have less power in the world claim they have the sovereign right to the power they now possess." He added in rolling Romanian intonation and syntax: "It cannot be for one nation sovereignty, and for other not."

The meeting was slipping, little by little, out of hand. People were beginning to turn to each other to comment privately on what was being said. The room buzzed with private conversations. Others responded openly, without waiting for recognition from the chair. It was only barely possible to hear chairman de Graaf reply, "In a transitional period you have to have a sliding scale of sovereignty."

Mussard raised his hand as his voice shot through the confusion. "Point of order, Mr. Chairman. Point of order. May I beg you respectfully to give the floor to those who ask for it and not to those who take it. Because otherwise it's simply unjust."

The confusion settled as delegates turned like school-boys to the chairman, who protested sheepishly, "But those who *take* it are not *given* it." Even in the hottest debate at the Dai Dong Conference good humor was never far beneath the often roiling surface.

But candor was harder to maintain than humor, even though the very conception of the conference was that independent voices would be free to speak openly in a way that delegates to UNCHE weren't. "Candor is the basis for this conference," Al Hassler declared. "We are not a conference representing states or individual communities. We are a conference of people (I assume—this is the basis on which we started) who recognize themselves as citizens of a world community, whose first loyalty is to the family of man (whatever that may mean). And I think we know what the problems are. The people who represent the third-world countries fear that if sovereignty is taken away they will have lost their last chance to control their own resources. But the people who come from the powerful industrialized nations are talking about something quite different. They're talking about the outmoded idea that nations have the right to determine every question in their own interest. And I think candor would require that we say: If you're not awfully careful, people from the third world, you're going to be caught in the same trap of national sovereignty that we have been in. And when you insist on sovereignty, it isn't going to be for the people you want it for; it's going to be for the elite in your country, and for the exploitation by the sovereignties in the powerful countries. We ought to be able to talk about these things here, precisely because we are committed to the idea of building a world that is human and that has respect for all human beings and that is not concerned with the profit of small groups."

In the end, it wasn't candor so much as haggling, compromise, and legerdemain that brought the conference to its final formulation on sovereignty in the declaration:

> The foreign investments, economic development and technological practices of . . . industrial states must be curbed and altered by the basic claim of a region's people to its resources. Use of these resources, however, should not be dictated by the accidents of geography, but must be allocated in such ways as to serve the needs of the world's people in this and future generations. The authority of any region's people over resources and environment must include the obligation to recognize that the environment is an indivisible whole, not subject to political barriers. The environment must be protected from avoidable pollution, destruction and exploitation from all sources.

War was the second extremely difficult issue for the Dai Dong Conference. Very simply, the struggle was between pacifists, who felt that the declaration must renounce war altogether, and nonpacifists, who, while abhorring war and denouncing imperialist aggression, wished the declaration to express clear and full support for wars of liberation.

War turned out to be a crucial issue for UNCHE too.

For even as the nations of the world gathered in Stockholm to save the environment from poisoning and collapse, the United States was pouring resources and energies and human lives into the calculated and atrocious destruction of Indochina. The mind has been numbed by the statistics of that war. It is quite powerless to deal with the tonnage of bombs rained by American planes on Indochina, which far exceeds that dropped in all other wars put together, by all sides. It is no better able to comprehend the more than 26 million bomb craters with which this tonnage has scarred the landscape.[1] Fifteen percent of the land of South Vietnam has been chemically defoliated. One million acres of crop and forest land have been scraped bare by giant bulldozers. The announced function of these "Rome Plows" is to "deny cover to the enemy," but their actual effect is utterly to destroy the fertility of cropland and the delicate ecological balance of the forest. As the land is laid waste, the people who have depended on soil and forest are made refugees, are forced into urban or pseudo-urban concentrations with their attendant pollution where they are themselves more easily controlled, and are no longer able to feed, shelter, and support the "enemy." Above all, as the United Nations Conference on the Human Environment proclaims in its very name, human beings are part of the environment, and it is primarily human beings the United States destroys, not only as an unavoidable consequence of political hostility, but through overt policies to maim, displace, and demoralize the civilian population. The atrocity at My Lai which the government now disavows is dwarfed by its avowed policies of carpet bombing, of "search-and-

[1] This estimate of 26 million bomb craters, covering a total area of 423,000 acres and representing a total displacement of about 3.4 billion cubic yards of earth is only for the period from 1965 to 1971, as reported in Arthur H. Westing and E. W. Pfeiffer, "The Cratering of Indochina," *Scientific American*, Vol. 226, No. 5 (May, 1972), pp. 20–29. To this estimate must be added the extensive cratering that has resulted from relentless massive bombing since 1971, which continues in Cambodia at this writing. See *The Effects of Modern Weapons on the Human Environment in Indochina* (Stockholm, June, 1972), available from the International Commission of Enquiry into U.S. Crimes in Indochina, Kungsgatan 24, S–111 35, Stockholm, Sweden.

destroy" missions, of "free-fire zones," of seeding civilian
areas with antipersonnel bombs. The latest nuance, which
came to light about the time of UNCHE, was the antipersonnel bomb with plastic shrapnel, designed not to kill
its victim but to be invisible to X-rays so that it cannot be
removed by surgery. It is a device whose purpose is indiscriminate torture of the human population. How could an
international assembly, convened to discuss the saving of
the environment, ignore the barbarous war in Indochina?

It couldn't. It tried. The United States did all it could
to force UNCHE's head into the sand. It couldn't. To begin
with, the press was full of what UNCHE was refusing to take
up, fixing it plainly in public view. The Swedes knew what
was on people's minds even if UNCHE pretended not to. All
those police were there, after all, primarily to guard against
expected fierce antiwar demonstrations. The ubiquitous
cops were a constant reminder of what the U.S. delegation
kept insisting was a nonissue. But the real bomb was
dropped on U.S. determination to keep discussion of the
war out of UNCHE by Olof Palme, prime minister of
Sweden, in his address to the second plenary session on
Tuesday, the sixth of June. He mentioned neither Vietnam
nor the United States by name, but his reference was
unmistakable. "The immense destruction brought about by
indiscriminate bombing, by large scale use of bulldozers and
herbicides is an outrage sometimes described as ecocide,
which requires urgent international attention. It is shocking
that only preliminary discussions of this matter have been
possible so far in the United Nations and at the conferences
of the International Committee of the Red Cross, where it
has been taken up by my country and others. We fear that
the active use of these methods is coupled by a passive
resistance to discussing them. We know that work for disarmament and peace must be viewed in a long perspective.
It is of paramount importance, however, that ecological warfare cease immediately."

Of course Palme is savvy enough to know that it isn't
"passive resistance," but political bludgeoning by the United
States that keeps the issues of the Indochina war and

ecocide out of those forums. Its own delegation had to be muzzled by the U.S. State Department. *The New York Times* reported on May 22, 1972, that all members of the U.S. delegation had "been instructed that they must support without question the official United States position on all the recommendations—totalling about 200—drawn up by the United Nations preparatory committee for conference discussion and action, even when they do not agree." Members of the Secretary of State's own advisory committee on the Stockholm conference charged that Russell Train and Christian Herter, Jr., leaders of the U.S. delegation, not only ignored, but refused even to discuss their recommendations with them. "The Administration," *The Times* reported, "hopes that some of the frustrations and disappointments of the scientists and environmental groups will be worked off at the Environment Forum that will be held concurrently with the two-week United Nations conference beginning June 5. . . . What does have the Administration and State Department deeply worried, however, is . . . that there will be demonstrations against United States bombing and defoliation in Vietnam." *The Times* opined hopefully that, "some Senators on the delegation . . . may balk at not being able to speak their minds even if they have to vote as instructed." But the administration knew its men. If there was any balking, it didn't show. All the public saw was harmony, impeccable manners, and Shirley's timeless smile.

The administration's delegation was angered by Palme's breach of diplomatic etiquette. "Yesterday the Prime Minister of Sweden took it upon himself to inject a highly emotional issue into the proceedings of the environmental conference," said Russell Train in his neat, gray suit. "The United States takes strong exception to these remarks, as Sweden is serving as the host government. . . . The charges of ecological warfare leveled by the Prime Minister are plainly directed at the United States. His environmental conscience is apparently unmoved by the naked aggression of others." Then Train struck his pose of the guileless, classic American, innocent of the sophistications of Old World politics, startled and saddened by this revelation of its machinations. "I am personally an environmentalist, not a politician," he said. "I wish to see the U.N. Conference on the Human Environment a success. I wish to see us work together in a spirit of positive cooperation for development and for global environmental protection." In Mr. Train's (read Washington's) sense of things, the conference could be a success only by limiting the agenda to the correct issues—those not embarrassing to the United States. "The injection of a highly charged issue by the Prime Minister can only do a disservice to this objective. The United States has continuously urged and sought full discussion and resolution of these issues in the proper fora. This Conference is not the place and the United States strongly objects to what it considers the gratuitous politicizing of our environmental discussions."

There was considerable speculation in the press that the United States might walk out of UNCHE in protest against the rudeness of its host. But Washington shrewdly understood that walking out would only sharpen the issue and force it more into the public view. "I certainly don't intend to walk out of this conference," Train told the press. "We expect to work within the conference and help make it a success." The next day, the U.S. delegation sent William Ruckelshaus, head of the Environmental Protection Administration, to a press conference to smooth things over. Ruckelshaus reiterated that the U.S. had no intention of walking out. It is quite natural for different people to have different opinions as to what constitutes environmental protection, he allowed. We have come here to listen. He added that Mr. Palme's speech was unfortunate, however, in that it threatened to divert attention from other important questions, for which preparations had been under way for two years. On the same day, responding to a reporter's question about environmental destruction in Vietnam, Shirley Temple Black put aside her disarming smile for a moment and replied earnestly, "The news is not all bad. I think it's one-sided in many cases."

Ruckelshaus ventured out once more into public confrontation on the war issue a week later, the evening before

UNCHE ended. He had been invited to represent the U.S. delegation in a panel debate at the Environment Forum, the U.N.-supported, semiofficial alternative conference paid for by the Swedish government to channel scientific and political criticism of UNCHE into harmless discussion. His presence was no small concession by the U.S. *The Nation* quoted Ross Vincent, a twenty-nine-year-old delegate, vice-president and research director of the Ecology Center of Louisiana, as saying, "There was an enormous amount of paranoia among the security people about whether the delegates should attend any of the alternative conferences going on." *The Nation* continued, "Dire warnings were whispered by the U.S. Embassy about the 'radical' doings at the Environment Forum, a U.N.-sponsored counter-conference that drew such wild-eyed folk as Margaret Mead and Barbara Ward. 'I guess they think anybody who opposes the U.S. position in Vietnam is a radical,' said Vincent, who finally convinced the delegation to meet with some nondelegate citizens after he had taken some VIPs to the forum to prove that they wouldn't be mugged."[2]

On the panel with Ruckelshaus were Margaret Mead, Barry Commoner, E. W. Pfeiffer, professor of zoology at the University of Montana and collaborator with Arthur Westing in studies of environmental destruction in Indochina, and Hans Göran Franck, lawyer and chairman of the Swedish Committee for Vietnam. The audience at the Environment Forum this particular evening hadn't come to talk about air pollution or ocean dumping or the green revolution. They had come to pin Ruckelshaus down on the war.

Ruckelshaus is the very image of the gentlemanly, clean-cut bureaucrat of the Nixon administration. Just a shade beefy, he parts his hair with tonic. And he is very, very polite. He had come as a reasonable man to discuss with other reasonable men and women whatever questions might reasonably, under the rubric of environment, be discussed. The Indochina war was not a reasonable subject.

[2] Lynn Langway and Jerry Edgerton, "The U.S. at Stockholm," *The Nation*, Vol. 215, No. 1 (July 10, 1972), p. 10.

He carried off his steadfast refusal to discuss it flawlessly for some two hours of challenges both from the other panelists and from members of the audience, who were invited to step to one of two microphones stationed on the floor and address questions to the panel. E. W. Pfeiffer presented Ruckelshaus with photographs of environmental destruction in Indochina, for his information, Pfeiffer told him. Ruckelshaus ignored the condescension, and accepted the photographs graciously. Questioner after questioner attacked bitterly Ruckelshaus's contention that the war issue was irrelevant to a discussion of the environment. He fielded all questions calmly, like a gentleman, never raising his voice, politely reiterating his governments "position" that an environmental conference was not the proper forum in which to debate the war. The meeting got pretty rowdy. Each new challenge was applauded and cheered, and each parry by Ruckelshaus snickered at and booed. After two hours even Republican Ruckelshaus, somewhere beneath that Brylcreem unruffleability, was touched by embarrassment. People just wouldn't let him put aside the horror of his government's policies, and you couldn't see, but you could sense that he was a decent man who somewhere inside was moved by the indignation of these people. Pfeiffer turned violently in his chair, grabbed the microphone in front of him, and glared down the table at Ruckelshaus. "Are you going to tell the President that everyone at the conference and everyone you met demanded U.S. withdrawal from Vietnam? Or are you going to tell him that everything was rosy at Stockholm?"

"I shall tell him," Ruckelshaus answered mildly, "that I was invited to a very interesting meeting, where there were a lot of people who seemed to regard the issues of war and the environment as one and the same." Until the Vietnam war is over, he added, "I see that we shall have trouble in convincing them that the U.S. is serious about [solving the problems that threaten the] environment." Hans Göran Franck stood and asked the audience to approve by vocal acclamation a resolution condemning the United States for its crimes of genocide and ecocide in Indochina. Ruckelshaus, however, slipped unobtrusively out the side way as a roar of approval went up in the hall.

U.S. efforts to defuse antiwar criticism at UNCHE didn't work. Many delegations expressed support for Palme's speech. Even the International Boy Scouts denounced "the deliberate destruction of the environment by warfare. The United States government's disgraceful war of ecocide in Indochina . . . should have been dealt with by this conference," declared their representative in an address to UNCHE's plenary.

On Saturday the tenth, Tang Ke, chairman of the Chinese delegation, told the plenary, "Our conference should strongly condemn the United States for their wanton bombings and shellings, use of chemical weapons, massacre of the people, destruction of human lives, annihilation of plants and animals, and pollution of the environment."

Gladwin Hill reported to *The New York Times* the flustered response of the U.S. delegation. "The vehemence of the Chinese attack, coming so soon after President Nixon's visit to China, appeared to take the United States by surprise. The United States delegation quickly asked for rebuttal time this afternoon, but nearly five hours later the American deputy chairman, Christian A. Herter Jr., puffed to the platform to report that the rebuttal was not yet ready. It was deferred until Monday. A hastily called United States news conference an hour and a half later was canceled at the last minute. United States sources indicated the problem had been in getting any sort of rejoinder cleared at a high level in Washington." When the rebuttal finally came, late in Monday's afternoon plenary session, it was again couched in conciliatory, rather than confrontational terms. Russell Train wore a daisy in his buttonhole as he read the brief statement to a hall largely abandoned by the bored, hungry delegates. It was "regrettable," he said, that China's address "was so inappropriately laden with political and ideological invective. Most of us here . . . are eager to work together in a spirit of reason and cooperation for international development and environmental protection, whatever our differences on other subjects may be. This objective will not be served by bringing into our deliberations highly charged issues extraneous to our agenda and impossible of solution at this forum."

The official U.S. line that the war was irrelevant had been carefully formulated and controlled behind the scenes by the Departments of State and Defense, which had produced a large, black policy "bible" to "guide" American delegates toward proper attitudes. "Matters of disarmament and testing of weapons should not be dealt with in a declaration on the human environment," the bible directed the delegation. "Defense had control of anything relating at all, in their view, to weapons or testing—their fine hand was everywhere," one U.S. delegate said.[3] The U.S. had originally vigorously supported the draft resolution on atomic testing, which banned testing in the atmosphere—which the U.S. doesn't do. But when New Zealand and Peru presented a broadened proposal, calling for an end to all testing, including underground testing—which the U.S. does do—its ardor suddenly cooled. Of course, nothing UNCHE passed was binding anyway, but the broadened resolution represented nevertheless an "embarrassment." It was supported so widely that the U.S. could not actively oppose it. "I guess we'll be abstaining," Christian Herter explained. "Our Defense Department would never go along with a 'yes' vote." France, which had scheduled atmospheric tests over Mururoa Atoll in the Pacific for a few weeks after the conference, and China, which explained that although she favored an end to nuclear armament, she had to continue testing for "defensive reasons," cast the only two votes openly against the resolution.

"Embarrassment" was, of course, what the United States was trying to avoid with its search for "peace with honor" in Indochina. Even after the "cease-fire," it has achieved neither peace nor honor, because the reality was never at issue, only the words, only the veneer of the pitchmen. Richard Nixon sold the image of disengagement while

[3] Ibid., p. 7.

he in fact escalated the air war, just as he called for U.N. condemnation of "international terrorism" even as he was bombing thc North Vietnamese "to their knees." If the U.S. was actually reversing its strategy and disengaging from the war, logic would suggest that it might confront Stockholm's antiwar demonstrators who were demanding the U.S. get out of Vietnam by saying, "We agree; we *are* getting out; now let's move on to other environmental matters we still need to discuss." But the appearance of rectitude and the maintenance of face mattered more than facts. Besides, when it came down to it, the U.S. didn't agree it should get out, wasn't really getting out, and thoroughly approved of what it had done there, though it couldn't say so. The fact was, and remains, that the destruction of Indochina by the U.S. military has been a critical part of a calculated and unrelenting strategy that the government has no intention of abandoning.

While the U.N. Conference was to skirt the issue of the Indochina war as irrelevant and to fiddle with the issue of nuclear weapons so as not to embarrass any of its sovereign member states, the issue of war flared openly in the Dai Dong Conference. But openness proved risky. Monday, the fifth of June, the day UNCHE began, had been scheduled as the final working day for the Independent Conference, but the issue of war threatened that schedule, threatened to delay publication the next day of Dai Dong's Independent Declaration. What was the conference going to declare?

One-time Marine Arthur Westing, still bristling with his boyish flat-top, though now professor of botany at Windham College, proposed the addition of a sentence that would condemn especially the strategy of ecocide in warfare. It was Westing's research carried out with E. W. Pfeiffer that had revealed the devastating impact of the craterization of Indochina as a result of U.S. saturation bombing. "A strategy of war that involves the intentional destruction of an adversary's natural resource base must be singled out for special proscription in any declaration on the environment."

Georgescu-Roegen objected. To issue a statement singling out nuclear or biological or chemical warfare, or—as in this case—ecocidal warfare, suggests that conventional warfare is all right, he argued. "I am opposed to singling out any kind of war in a declaration against war. I think that we should call for the total abolition of war, in all forms. We should protest war—*period*. All was is bad, and we should make the statement against war categorical. War is war—*period*. In all forms. We cannot imagine at this time what other devilish things the human mind may invent in the future—sterilization, idiotization through chemicals. . . . We should not try to specify any kind of war and say that this is a little war, and that is a big war."

Taghi Farvar expressed opposition to a categorical statement against war, such as Georgescu-Roegen had suggested, or, for that matter, to a statement advocating total disarmament. Again, a hostile chorus: "Why?"

"Why am I opposed to a statement against war, period? Because I think," Taghi replied, "there are certain wars that have to be fought. I would never tell the Vietnamese people to stop fighting a war today. Given the historical moment when this declaration is being made, and the conference [UNCHE] which is otherwise ignoring the issues of war (particularly the wars that are affecting us now: Southeast Asia, Angola, Mozambique, etc.), I think we have an obligation to make a special point of unconditional support of the liberation movements. . . . We must decide whether we are on the side of liberation movements, or against them."

Eraj countered that basic to the idea of Dai Dong is the transcendence of war as a solution to human conflict. The Menton Statement had already called for the abolition of war. Hassler, who had served several years at Lewisburg Penitentiary as a conscientious objector during World War II, picked up on this theme. "I think we should be reminded," he said, "of the context in which this group has been called together. The nature of Dai Dong in its own commitment, its own approach, has been very clear from the start. It was made clear to everybody who was invited to attend this conference. It included the necessity of speaking to the eradication of war—*period*. If we are going to become involved in political discussions of which wars are good and which wars are bad, we are back in the trap of the attitudes which Dai Dong itself is committed to escape. We would be totally in contradiction to the fundamental concepts of Dai Dong if we begin to say we give complete support to a war of liberation here, a war of liberation there. We have said that men must get rid of the business of using war to achieve justice, to solve their problems, and so on. We contradict our own basis if we take that kind of position. I think we should vote that down absolutely."

Bolivian Schütt-Mogro responded that no one at this conference would say he was against the French or American revolutions. The present liberation movements are also movements for new societies, and they must as such be supported.

"On the same basis," answered Georgescu-Roegen, "we may say that since we had an atomic war in history, we ought to support one in the future. We are not here to extrapolate from what was bad in the past," he added passionately. "We are here to set down the principles of a world of our dreams—not of our past suffering."

But Schütt-Mogro insisted on the distinction between institutionalized violence, violence perpetrated by oppressive governments and exploitative colonial powers, and legitimate revolutionary violence, which is pursued only to achieve justice. We must change the political systems by which the world is governed if we are truly to avert war, for it is these existing systems that produce it. His earlier statement, which he proposed to be added to the declaration, argued in essentially Marxist terms the human right to fight oppression: "We recognize the inalienable right of peoples to struggle materially and spiritually in order to achieve their liberation from the present oppressive systems at both the national and international levels. We believe that peace will become a reality only when the present exploitative and oppressive systems are replaced by economic, social and political systems which will result in a classless society and a balanced development on a global scale."

But this statement had been unacceptable to those who denied that the way to abolish war is more war. "There is no way to peace," A. J. Muste, past head of the Fellowship of Reconciliation once put it; "peace is the way." Conspicuous by their absence from this discussion of war were the two Vietnamese, Thich Nhat Hanh, and Cao Ngoc Phuong, formerly professor of biology at the Universities of Saigon and Hue. Both live in exile for their resistance to the war at home; both are members of the little-known Vietnamese Buddhist Peace Delegation in Paris, which represents the so-called third-force position that the first priority in Indochina is not political victory, but an end to the killing. During the early years of Lyndon Johnson's escalation of the war, the Buddhists' nonviolent resistance and self-sacrifice made a major impact on the peace movement in the West. Now they have been all but forgotten, when not actually maligned by those who argue that the war must be fought through to genuine liberation—that peace on terms less than victory is surrender. Nhat Hanh in his brown monastic robes, and Phuong, in her straight brown dress, open at the sides, over black silk pants, were rarely caught up in conference wrangling. Yet they seemed often the deep eye at the center of the storm. At an earlier plenary session Phuong had asked quietly, so that one strained to hear her, that the declaration express support for revolutionary movements like the Buddhists', which work for change without weapons, without violence. Now, Nhat Hanh and Phuong were absent from the debate on war. They had returned to Paris suddenly on receiving word of the death of Nhat Hanh's former student and close friend Thich Tanh Van. Tanh Van's small car, returning to Saigon from relief work in the countryside, had been hit by a U.S. Army truck. He had been refused admittance to an army hospital, and had died of his injuries two days later.

Schütt-Mogro offered a compromise. It was broad enough, he felt, to allow both sides of the issue to endorse it. "People have the exclusive right," it ran, "to determine the nature of their own social system. Despite our general opposition to war we also recognize the right of people to choose the necessary means for achieving this."

Mussard was blunt. "I have the impression that this statement confuses the issue. I realize that the purpose is to achieve a compromise, but personally I prefer clarity. If we mean that we recognize the right of people to oppose violence with violence when they are forced to (and this is, I guess, what we mean), why don't we say it frankly? Why do we try to confuse the issue in a statement which each person can understand as he likes? I don't like violence, but I am prepared to accept a clear statement. This one is not clear."

"I'm talking to Mussard's proposal," replied Hassler, "that this be made a straight statement that people have the right to strike back militarily. I wouldn't write this the way Mr. Mogro has written it. I think we get caught in a dilemma. It's very hard for those of us who do not live in an exploited and oppressed society (at least not as much as some societies are) to say, 'no, it is wrong to struggle, it is wrong to fight the enemy, the oppressor, to use violence in that situation.' We recognize the role which our nations have played in the oppression, and the responsibility which therefore rests with us. But that does not bring me to the point of saying that I recognize the right of anybody to kill anybody else in the achievement of the objectives that they want. I do not. I think practically as well as morally it is self-defeating, because what happens—particularly in these days of concentration of power in the great nations—what happens when you fight is that you get napalmed and bombed and all the innocent and uninvolved noncombatants are the ones who are killed. And they don't choose for themselves. It seems to me that we recognize that violence *is* going to occur, that people *are* going to struggle, that we are in sympathy with those who are struggling for justice and freedom, and we recognize their right to do so, and that if they have no other means, they are going to struggle violently. Our position, it seems to me, is that to the very maximum extent possible, those struggles ought to be carried on nonviolently, and they have to be carried on

nonviolently as well by those of us in the imperialistic
countries in alliance with the others. But our ultimate judg-
ment from the perspective of Dai Dong is that we have got
to get rid of the process of killing other people in order to
achieve justice—that we have got to get rid of the killing of
people, the organized killing of people, even if it is claimed
to be—as it always is—for justice. There never was an
unjust war—every war that's ever been fought was fought
for justice as the people who fought it defined justice, or
for the defense of their rights. Somehow or other we have
to say that we have come to that moment in history when
we will either get rid of this process of defending our own
positions, solving our conflicts, attaining our own ends by
killing other people, or we will *all* perish. Now it's very
difficult for us as people from the industrialized world to
come to some formulation of that sort together with people
who are coming out of the nations which we have been
involved in oppressing. So we try to find a compromise. But
you can't push us too far. And you're not going to push me
to the point of saying, 'It's all right for people to go around
killing other people in order to attain justice,' because I
don't think it is all right."

As those who represented the radical third-world view
saw it, Hassler was missing the point. "You don't simply
shoot the other person because you don't agree with them,"
said Jurgenne Primavera. "You shoot him because he is
shooting at you—which is the case in very oppressive societies in the developing countries. There is no other option.
And there is no other option for us than to support liberation
movements."

It was nine o'clock. At nine o'clock each evening tea
was served. And having counted earlier in the day how
many guests to expect for evening tea, and having prepared
just the right number of sandwiches and cakes, and having
set them out neatly on little trays with doilies on them, the
dour management would be impatient with guests who did
not appear on time for tea. Two girls in dainty serving
aprons would be waiting expectantly behind the counter.
But at nine o'clock of the evening before the Independent

Declaration was to be presented to the press, the conference seemed far as ever from agreement on a statement about war, not to speak of population, which had already been deferred till the next morning. People would just go on talking, it seemed, passionately seeking to persuade the others of their various, irreconcilable positions till the cows came home—if cows ever do come home in that dreamy midsummer twilight. Mild-mannered Hannes de Graaf looked sternly at the conference members sitting around the room at tables arranged in an open square and delivered an ultimatum. "These are the alternatives," he said, raising his voice above the once more steadily rising confusion. "Within ten minutes you find a compromise—you don't take stands, you find a compromise, you all agree on it within ten minutes—or we drop the subject from the declaration altogether. The short time we have left is to find a compromise, not to speak anymore."

Fully an hour and a half earlier, Jens Brøndum, the supercharged deputy director of Dai Dong in Europe, whose ambitious arrangements for the conference in Stockholm laid the groundwork for its success, had come into the meeting with his own compromise statement. He apologized for interrupting the discussion, and for being unable to stay, since he was due back in Stockholm to introduce Dai Dong's public evening with Jun Ui and the Minamata victims. Although it was edited (rewritten) for the final version of the declaration later that night, the statement was now, in the face of de Graaf's ineluctable ultimatum, quickly adopted by acclamation of the entire conference. "We feel deep solidarity with those who, because of the violence of their oppressors, are fighting for liberty. At the same time, we state the urgent necessity of finding non-violent means to solve social and political conflicts if this world is not to be the victim of ecocidal war." There was much applause, relief, and just a little self-congratulation.

"Mr. Chairman, Mr. Chairman," called out Satish Kumar over the settling applause. "This conference is very speedy. You gave us ten minutes; we took ten seconds."

"I thank you," the chairman assured the group facetiously, "from the bottom of my heart." Gratefully, with only the population question left to settle, the conference adjourned for tea.

The population question, left in a deadlock, had been put in the hands of the editorial "committee" of one, Dorothy Maas, in consultation with the authors of four of the five statements on population proposed for adoption by the plenary. Between this evening's tea and lunch the next day, Tuesday, the declaration had to be typed and reproduced in final form for distribution to the press. The plan was for Dorothy Maas to put together a statement, incorporating and combining the major points of each of the contending statements—a statement that would miraculously satisfy everyone. The miracle didn't come off.

Why was compromise so difficult? Actually, the lines of battle had been drawn long before Stockholm. It is most notorious as an ostensibly scientific dispute between Paul Ehrlich and Barry Commoner. Ehrlich's thesis in *The Population Bomb*, roughly put, is that population is a major key to the environmental crisis.[4] At the end of the eighteenth century the Reverend Thomas Malthus had warned of the inevitable crush of an exponentially expanding population. Malthus saw quite simply that while population expands exponentially—doubling, he thought, every twenty-five years—the land on which that population's food is produced expands, if at all, only arithmetically. "Land can be added to laboriously, but the rate of progress is slow and hesitant," Robert Heilbroner explains;"unlike population, land does not breed."[5]

In some nonindustrialized countries—India is the prime example—the Malthusian nightmare of famine and disease has come to pass. In the industrialized nations, however, two factors primarily have forestalled its arrival. First is the so-called demographic transition, the fact that a decline in the birth rate appears to accompany industrialization. Sec-

---

[4] Paul Ehrlich, *The Population Bomb* (New York: Ballantine Books, 1968).
[5] Robert L. Heilbroner, *The Worldly Philosophers*, 4th rev. ed. (New York: Simon & Schuster, 1972), p. 82.

ond is the fact that progress in agriculture has continuously increased the productivity of land, so that even though land has not expanded exponentially, production has been able to keep pace with population increase. Ehrlich's position is that we can buy no more time. As population increases exponentially, so does the burden that this increasing population places on finite resources and on the global environment's finite carrying capacity for waste. Moreover, the exponentially increasing competition for the world's limited wealth assures the widening of the gap between rich and poor and the heightening of social and international conflict. Resource depletion, pollution, poverty, hunger, malnutrition, and war are thus the inevitable consequences of unchecked population growth. If the explosion can be slowed and eventually reversed, Ehrlich argues, the problems of pollution, hunger, and injustice can also be solved. But population control in some form is a necessary condition for the continued survival and well-being of man and his environment.

From the opposing trench Commoner argues, in *The Closing Circle*, for example, that social, economic, and political systems—not population—are the cause of the environmental crisis. It is the system of production that makes waste and pollution and spiraling industrial growth necessary, that bases the wealth of a few on the exploitation of the many, that is motivated by profit or the drive for power instead of the need to assure healthy, meaningful lives for all the world's people, and that is the root of the population explosion itself. Commoner argues on the basis of the demographic transition that the solution to the crisis of the environment, including overpopulation, is a social revolution, which would have the effect of raising the quality of life for the billions of the world's people. If that occurred, population would stabilize of itself, as it has already begun to do in the United States and Western Europe, without programs of population control. In the meantime, such programs are at worst genocidal, and at best diversionary from the real economic and political bases of the crisis.

The controversy is no mere dispassionate difference of

scientific opinion. One Dai Dong Conference participant called it uncharitably "a violent debate, really, between two people who want to be emperor of ecology in the United States." But the seam of violence runs deeper than the personal ambitions (whatever they may be) of these two men, who only happen to have come to represent the opposing sides. The real heat is generated by politics, not personality, and it is enough to frizzle, not just fry, a metaphorical egg. As an ecologist, Ehrlich does not maintain that population is the only problem, nor does Commoner deny that it is any part of the problem at all. But the issue has overflowed the realm of pure science. The positions of Ehrlich and Commoner have been reduced by partisans to the either/or of politics, and the men themselves, alternately embattled and on the attack, have not always stuck singlemindedly to scientific dispassion. Nor should they, necessarily, science being at least as political in its implications as anything else, and scientists being also men and women with passions, and responsible citizens too.

The image stirred in most of us in the industrialized West by *the population explosion* might better be expressed as a nightmare sea of desperate brown and yellow faces, in which we and our prosperous neighbors (Bill on his riding mower, Jim and Nancy from the swim club, our kids and the kids next door putt-putting on minibikes) thrash about horribly and drown. Statistics that prove our imminent demise mathematically may leave us cold. But this vision touches us. Thus Ehrlich was touched. *The Population Bomb* opens with a grim description of how, after having understood the population crisis intellectually for a long time, Ehrlich suddenly came to understand it emotionally as well. The moment came in a dilapidated taxi which was returning Ehrlich and his wife and daughter to their hotel one miserably hot night in Delhi, India.

> The seats were hopping with fleas. The only functional gear was third. As we crawled through the city, we entered a crowded slum area. The temperature was well over 100, and the air was a haze of dust and smoke. The streets seemed alive with people. People eating, people

washing, people sleeping. People visiting, people arguing, and screaming. People thrusting their hands through the taxi window, begging. People defecating and urinating. People clinging to buses. People herding animals. People, people, people, people. As we moved slowly through the mob, hand horn squawking, the dust, noise, heat, and cooking fires gave the scene a hellish aspect. . . . All three of us were, frankly, frightened. It seemed that anything could happen. . . . Old India hands will laugh at our reaction. We were just overprivileged tourists, unaccustomed to the sights and sounds of India. Perhaps, but since that night I've known the *feel* of over-population.[6]

Nowhere is our deep-seated racism more obvious than in these attitudes. It isn't we who are exploding, it's them— all those hungry, sweating, dark-skinned people. When we speak of population control, we mean population control in Latin America or China, not Holland or Belgium, although these are the most densely populated countries in the world. We cite the staggering rate of population growth in India, and ignore the fact that each American consumes twenty times more than the average Indian and puts fifty times more waste into the environment. We cite the demographic transition and the declining rate of population growth in industrialized countries, and ignore the exponentially exploding consumption of resources and energy in those countries. It is not so much the undernourished and deprived masses of Indians who may engulf us apocalyptically tomorrow as it is we who are starving and asphyxiating them today by our inordinate demand for ever-greater consumption and waste. People in the third world know our attitudes, and look upon proposals for population control—even well-intentioned ones—with justifiable cynicism. Ehrlich advocated in *The Population Bomb* the tying of foreign aid to the institution in a country of population-control programs, and that criterion has in fact been used by the World Bank in issuing development loans to third-world countries.

The debate in the Dai Dong Conference was not

[6] Ehrlich, *Population Bomb,* pp. 15–16.

between supporters of Ehrlich and Commoner, although
their positions serve to focus the issue. Rather, it was between those who, as ecologists, felt obliged to identify over-
population as one of many factors degrading the environment, and those who, whatever their ecological judgments,
felt it politically unacceptable to do so. To advocate population control in any form, the latter would argue, is to play
into the hands of the imperialists.

UNCHE faced the same difficulty, and solved it
ostrich-fashion. Population was not on the agenda.[7] "The
United Nations has had an interest in population," Conrad
Istock observed, "for a very long time. In fact the history
goes back over twenty years when Sir Julian Huxley was
pleading with the United Nations to get going on the population problem. And it has never been successful." Dai
Dong must do better, he urged. "I think it's incumbent on
us somewhere in the declaration to really suggest a course of
action at this point. I think it's regrettable that under the
present circumstances of confusion and diverse opinion over
population that the U.N. is in fact (at least at the Stockholm
Conference) withdrawing some of its expressed concern
over population growth."

Donald Chant of Canada prefaced his reading of an
ad hoc population group's draft statement by admonishing
the plenary not to drop population from the declaration and
pretend, like UNCHE, that it was a nonissue.

> Human population growth cannot continue indefinitely
> in a finite environment. Therefore, rational debate on
> the matter of population can only be addressed to
> whether or not a problem of overpopulation exists today
> and, if not, when it may be expected to reach crisis
> proportions. The matter of population may be viewed
> from different aspects: space, the supply of finite re-
> sources, or food, for example. At this moment in time,
> the planet is not able to provide sufficient food and other
> resources for the present population of 3½ billion
> people, and therefore, the planet may be considered to

[7] Instead, population is to be the subject of a separate U.N. conference in 1974.

be overpopulated with respect to our ability to provide for ourselves. Undoubtedly, certain steps can be taken to improve this ability, but to continue to increase population is simply to gamble that these steps will be fully successful in a short space of time and to defer the time when eventually population will have to be controlled. On a global basis, there is no virtue in increasing population and it is folly to test the ultimate carrying capacity of our planet by trial and error. There will be a very long lead time to stabilizing population, and despite our best efforts during that time the world population may double or even treble. We may well err and discover that we have allowed our population to exceed this carrying capacity, which would create human misery and death on an unimaginable scale.

No known technology can substitute for primary biological production. The potential of our planet for the biological production of food is limited and cannot be raised beyond a certain absolute level. Efforts to increase production are today to a great extent carried out at the expense of the very basis of our future productivity; we are spending our capital.

There is, consequently, a limit to the population that our planet can feed, and particularly feed without at the same time lowering its productive potential. The present day population is barely fed at the expense of future generations.

We believe population is one of the key ecological factors and that today it is greatly aggravated by the consumption of resources. Therefore, it is particularly acute in developed countries and the initial burden of population control logically must fall on those countries where there is an emphasis on consumption. However, because most of the world's peoples seem to be dedicated to development and increased consumption, the burden of population control will fall on all members of the world community. In our view, development has not stopped population growth; it merely slows it and delays the crisis. Global population control must be closely associated with resource redistribution and with the free movement of people.

Developed countries must be urged to perfect acceptable methods of population control and to offer them to other countries that wish to regulate their population size and want to use them. Population control must not be imposed on nations that resist it, though we believe that ultimately it is essential for survival of our global system.

Without population stabilization we can never achieve a stable global system, and the other Dai Dong recommendations and principles cannot be successful.

Mussard objected to the sentence in the first paragraph which stated that the planet is not able to provide sufficient food and other resources for the present population of three and a half billion people. It is not the planet, but our social organizations, he argued, that are unable to provide it. The planet is indeed able to provide sufficient food, but *does* not. We even have the technology, but we misuse it.

"What I think we mean," replied Fred Knelman, a member of the ad hoc group, "is not that we can't find the technology to adequately feed, clothe, and house the three and a half billion people which constitute the present population, but that as long as population grows, there will be a continuing stress on the ecosphere, and that no matter how much time we buy through technology, at some point in the future, at some level of population, we will reach another crisis. And therefore we are saying, let us try to solve the problems of feeding, clothing, and maintaining the health of the three and a half billion people; let's not gamble on a technology that may or may not in time provide the answers we are seeking. That's the sense of this. The sense isn't that technology isn't able to do it, but that we are gambling by continuing to have population grow."

Mussard insisted on his point: "I do not mean that it is purely a question of technology. It's a question of social organization." And this was indeed the focus of his own proposed statement:

It is quite clear that the human population cannot grow indefinitely in a finite environment with finite resources. But as long as resources are wasted, as they manifestly are, it will remain an intellectual fraud to emphasize exclusively or even mainly the problem of population growth as if this was the source of all evils. (There is obviously a confusion in many people's minds between over-crowding and population.) The fact that some urban areas grow like cancers should not serve as a pretext to divert attention from the real task of our generation, which is to achieve proper management of resources and space. In other words, before claiming that our home (the earth) is too small, we should put some order in it. At present the oceans, lakes and lands are being poisoned and the capacity of the earth to produce food under ecologically sound conditions is not properly exploited. Those nations that are mainly responsible for this state of affairs have certainly no right to recommend population stabilizing policies to the hungry peoples. Such policies may be implemented by these peoples as a measure of urgency, but this is their own affair.

Mussard's draft recognized population as a factor in the global budget, but argued that priorities demand that we direct our attention and energies elsewhere. He clarified his major contention that population can only be considered in the context of consumption: "In order that the population problem be put in the right place—not under the table, but in the right place—let's assume that the population is stabilized today at its present level, three and a half billion. What I want to show is that it is a problem of standards. If we take the American standard of living as a goal, as an ideal, and we accept the current ideology of development which implicitly presumes that the developing countries should sooner or later reach the same standard as the Americans, say within a hundred years, and if we also accept the current ideology of economic growth, say four percent a year, then arithmetically, with a stable population, the consumption of resources would be increased by a factor of fifty—that's the order of magnitude. Now whether we stabilize the population at the present level, or we allow for it even to double—well, it's certainly a factor. But comparing population with consumption is comparing the factor two with the factor fifty. That's why I say that we must have the courage to put the emphasis on the priority. Our present ideologies are unacceptable, even if we stabilize the population. If we accept this ideology of growth and welfare based on American standards, we ought to advocate the *reduction* of the population by a factor of fifty within a hundred years. This is what we must say, honestly."

"Gandhi once said," commented de Graaf, " 'There is enough for everybody's need, but not enough for everybody's greed.' And we are in the awkward position at the moment that the *greedy* are saying there is not enough for everybody's *need*. This is unjust, and I feel the justification of those who protest. When you speak of population it is a question of priorities, a question of context."

"You cannot add a Buddhist monk to an American millionaire and say this makes too many people on the earth," added Mussard. "If all the people of the world lived like Buddhist monks the population problem would look quite different. I'm not suggesting that we should do that—I simply want to draw attention to something nonsensical in these statistics. It all depends what we do. If we live more modestly, there is plenty of room on the earth."

A third draft was proposed by Georgescu-Roegen. His statement reflected the special perspective of his economic analysis, in which he applies the second law of thermodynamics, the entropy law, to the economic process. The entropy law states that any closed system tends irreversibly toward disorganization. Put another way, the energy differential within any system, its dynamic potential, tends toward equilibrium. The water that turns a mill wheel, for instance, has energy potential only until it reaches equilibrium at the bottom of the wheel's turning. To keep the wheel going requires more water at the top. A spring kept wound gradually loses its resilience, and thus its potential energy. Air of differing temperatures in a room mingles toward equilibrium until the temperature throughout the room is uniform.

Matter and energy cannot be destroyed, but they are transformed from low entropy to high entropy, or from free energy, available for use, to bound energy, inert or inaccessible. A lump of coal, for instance, is organized low entropy, free and available for energy. We can store it until we need its energy, then we can burn it. Once it has been burned, however, much of its substance is dispersed (thus disorganized), and the cinder, which remains visibly intact, cannot be burned for energy again. Similarly, an iron tool is a highly organized piece of matter which tends more and more to be transformed through abrasion and oxidation, and to be dispersed as tiny particles of iron and rust into the environment in a useless (because irretrievable) form. Recycling does not reverse the entropic process, since the input of matter/energy required necessarily exceeds output.

The second law of thermodynamics is stated for the physical universe; the economic process, which takes place within the physical realm, must be subject to its laws, and the insight that this is so must in turn qualify our conception of economics. If we look just at the material aspect, we see that the economic process consists ultimately in transforming valuable natural resources (low entropy) into useless waste (high entropy). The real output of the economic process is not material, however, for the material process is not pursued for its own sake, but for the sake of what Georgescu-Roegen calls "an immaterial flux: the enjoyment of life." Thus, the material process is, strictly speaking, the *cost* of that immaterial flux, and realizing that, we ought to confront the question, what are we buying at that cost? What is the *benefit*?

> From the material viewpoint all life processes, including that of mankind, in the ultimate analysis consist of a transformation of material resources into waste. Some of this waste is harmful to future life, but all is irrevocable waste that can no longer support life. Any economic activity, not only that directed toward economic development, therefore produces waste. Harmful waste (pollution) may be minimized, not eliminated, through improved processes, but this improvement has its limitations and also its cost. Furthermore, the natural resources at the disposal of mankind are strikingly anti-

symmetrical: those in the bowels of the earth can be used by mankind almost at will, but they represent only an infinitesimal amount relative to the flow of solar radiation reaching our planet over billions of years to come. And over this flow mankind has no control. Given this discrepancy, the mechanization of agriculture, although now responding to the immense pressure for food of an increased population, represents a move against the most elementary ecological interest of the human species. Not before this population has, through continuous and persistent efforts, been brought down to a level capable of being maintained by non-mechanized agriculture, can mankind consider itself freed from the most dangerous ecological trap in its history. It is because the rate of flow of the solar energy caught by the earth is an unalterable datum for mankind and because the earth-bound resources are so scarce that the size of the population at any one time is a most critical element of the ecological problem. For the same reasons, objects of war, of luxury, or those that feed that disease of the mind we call "fashion" represent the greatest waste for the human species as a whole. Every Cadillac and every Zim mean so many fewer plough shares for the future generations. And since these generations cannot bid now for resources we must seek their protection outside the market. Mankind must be trained to hear at any time the loud cries for food, water, and air of the future generations.

Because population was so sensitive an issue, many people, seeing in the statement what they expected to find rather than what was actually there, objected to the assertion that "the size of the population at any one time is *the* most critical element of the ecological problem." Actually, the assertion is simply that it is "*a* most critical element of the ecological problem," but even saying that much went too far for many. Georgescu-Roegen explained his position that, of course there were many other environmental problems besides population, but that all others are problems only by virtue of the size of population. That is, the source of socioeconomic problems behind the environmental crisis is scarcity, and scarcity has meaning only in relation to population size.

But Jurgenne Primavera, looking at the question not theoretically, but from the practical viewpoint of the individual human being in a country like her own, objected on different grounds. "Hopefully, we are making this statement not for the press, but for the whole world. And when you look at the whole world, you see that more than half are in the third world. So let's address this, say, to the Filipino farmer. When you say that population is the critical issue . . . O. K., you tell a Filipino farmer who earns one hundred dollars per annum—you tell him that if he has only two children instead of six or seven or eight or ten, his life will improve. Now if he does have only two children, will he earn more than one hundred dollars per annum? No. His earnings remain at one hundred dollars. Why? Because of the existing system of feudal landlords. When you say, 'Mankind must be trained to hear at any time the loud cries for food, water, and air of future generations,' I say, how about the cries for food, water, and air of the *present* generation? The poverty that exists?"

Taghi Farvar took up the attack. "Perhaps it would be fair to say that population is *an* element in the global system. I'm not sure it deserves any greater emphasis than that. I think we have enough data, enough facts to show that if our point of departure is the environmental crisis, the population factor has in fact very little to do with it. The nature of the technology, the way the goods that we want are produced, has a far greater impact than the numbers of people per se. I don't think that is a disputable fact any more. The nature of the economic system that is the cause of the technological system is the critical issue, and issues such as distribution, the nature of the exploitative systems that have caused the population problem in most of the world in the first place. . . . There is no reason why we should put the highest priority, or even an equally high priority on the population factor, when history shows that this element can be taken care of if the priority is put on the goods and how they are distributed. So I think meaningful development, meaning real per capita increase, which will have to come first of all by redistribution of what there is, ought to be the main emphasis."

"My statement does not exclude anything that you say," Georgescu-Roegen replied. "I said that if these social and economic differences did not exist, the population problem would not present itself in the way in which we are confronted with it today. This does not say that population is the only problem."

"I don't think anyone argues that population is *the most important* factor," added Henry Regier, who consistently argued a systems approach to understanding the environmental crisis. "I personally don't believe there *is* a most important factor, except regionally and temporarily."

"It's also not a question of absolutes," put in Donald Chant. "We're not talking about population stabilization *or* social change. Nor are we talking about social change without population stabilization. We're talking about the whole thing together. There *is* no one solution; there is a complex of solutions. I have the uneasy feeling that we're beginning to fall into the trap of absolutism by saying it's got to be this, or it's got to be that."

Taghi Farvar submitted his own draft, which recognized the existence of a population problem, but stressed its interrelatedness with socioeconomic and political problems, and questioned the effectiveness of programs of population control.

> The question of population is intrinsically inseparable from the question of access to resources. A true improvement in the conditions of living of the people of developing countries would go further in stabilizing population growth than programmes of population control. Population is not a single global or biological problem, but one which has a complex interrelationship with the social, economic and natural environments of man. Recognizing that in the industrialized countries the mode of production of economic goods is a much larger contributor to

the environmental crisis than population growth, it is clear that the emphasis must be on changing the modes of production, which, we believe, implies a change in the socio-economic systems governing the means of production.

In a second paragraph, Farvar went on to suggest that the history of imperialist exploitation of developing countries is the real cause of population problems. "The redistribution of resources on a global level is an unconditional prerequisite for correcting this historic process," his statement concluded. Like the others, Farvar's statement emphasized the centrality of inordinate consumption in industrialized countries. But Conrad Istock pointed out another horn of the dilemma of population stabilization and redistribution of wealth. It is perfectly true that consumption in the industrialized countries, and especially in the U.S., is grossly inordinate, and constitutes oppression of the deprived people of the world. Justice cries out for more equitable distribution of wealth. Yet the disheartening irony is that we are locked into the inequity. If, for example, the population in the industrialized nations fails to increase at the expected rate (a rate everyone agrees is catastrophic in the long run), the nonindustrialized countries which depend for their marginal subsistence on sales of raw materials simply suffer all the more. "The world is presently structured," said Istock, "so that there are in fact people in India dependent today on my consuming something. Here's the choice: one more child in Istock's family, or not. O.K.? If the child happens, then what the child does is to increase the rate of flow of raw materials to North America. That rate of flow *might* have gone somewhere else. But if the system can't respond so fast as to divert it usefully to the enrichment of someone else's life, then it can have the opposite effect. Because now there's no sale at all, so someone in an undeveloped country who was counting on a few marginal dollars coming to him by selling his raw materials to the U.S. just lost a customer. Because it wasn't born."

The real crux of the controversy was population control as public policy. In the end it came to this: there were those who saw population control *in some form* as an inescapable part of the complex solution to the contemporary predicament of mankind, while others felt that to consent to population control *in any form* was to open a sinister box of genocide and oppression. Fred Knelman tried, but failed, to reconcile these two irreconcilable positions with still another draft, which recognized both ecological principle and political reality. "There need be no conflict," it ran in part, "between the affirmation of a population factor and the most pressing need for rapid social change to overcome the gross inequalities that arise from the present state of maldistribution. In economically developed societies the levels of consumption create a major global burden of pollution and resource depletion and it is on these countries that the onus of population limitation and consumption reduction must be placed. Methods of population limitation and consumption reduction in these countries must in no way burden the poor and deprived who already suffer a maldistribution within these countries. Again there need be no conflict between these two principles." But there was.

Each new draft statement handed out to the conference was received with instinctive dismay, tinged with the wistful hope that this would finally satisfy the insatiable. Another paper! There had been draft declarations and amendment proposals and minutes and statements and proclamations; there were newspapers to follow and clippings from newspapers; there were leaflets and handbills and cards and petitions—papers, papers stuck into your hand wherever you went in Stockholm. At night you'd sheepishly pull a dozen or two out of your pockets and pretend, at least, to read them, or read snatches of them, because what a waste of resources otherwise! You'd look for something to wrap in the paper, a spill to wipe, a place in a book to mark. It was worse at UNCHE, where you were dealing after all with professionals. There were press tables and cubbyholes and baskets and information booths with piles of pamphlets and papers and press releases with words on them like armies of ants. Each word in the mouth of a diplomat, each bureaucratic syllable uttered was instantly transformed to paper. The whole conference, in fact, happened in silence, only paper spewing out of the delegates' opening and closing mouths. Buckets of paper. The mere sight of the print set the eyes to spinning, the temples to pounding—an infection whose worst symptom was that eyes and reeling brain could not trust the perverse hand, which, if paper wasn't thrust into it, would itself reach out for it, snatch it from a table, yet one more pamphlet or splendidly illustrated brochure or universal and ultimate manifesto of absolute human rights.

Debate dragged on Monday night out at Graninge, Tuesday's press conference looming ever closer, but consensus remained tied in this tangle of positions on population control. In desperation the Gordian knot was hacked at by putting the problem of formulation into the hands of the editorial "committee" and the ad hoc consultants. But it wasn't, as it turned out, a clean stroke.

"Just for the record," Jurgenne Primavera said sternly when this solution to the impasse had been adopted, "I could not attempt to change what has been decided on, but just for the record, I would like to express the feeling of people in the third world that all these conferences, all these meetings that emanate from the developed world, coming from the white man, do not say anything to the brown man, to the black man, but look at the probem only through the eyes of the white man."

There was some confusion over just what *had* been decided on. Taghi Farvar asked for the floor. "Referring back to Miss [sic] Primavera's statement—this declaration must speak, I feel, not only to the ecological judgments. . . . I'd like to point out that it's a question of the destiny of most of the people of the world you're talking about. And this committee that you propose to meet with Mrs. Maas—I see I guess about two Americans, one European . . ."

"There are *no* Americans," Canadians Chant and Knelman burst out in unison. Then Chant added, with a good deal of satisfaction, "*You're* the only American we know of."

Farvar explained that he was not objecting to the intentions or the capabilities of the Westerners on the committee, but to what he saw as the relative absence of third-world perspective. But chairman de Graaf brushed aside his objection. "This is absolutely out of order. Those people who have shown their concern, and who have worked at documents are going to be consulted. It has nothing to do with what nation they belong to." Farvar hadn't flinched in the face of a good deal of hostility over the past few days, but he seemed tired now, and took this rebuke hard. He buried his face in his hands a moment. Then he turned to Jurgenne Primavera, whispered something, and left the room.

By the time the plenary session gathered Tuesday morning after breakfast, almost everyone knew that hours of often bitter late night/early morning squabbling had not, after all, produced a statement on population. It had produced two statements. Unable to compromise with each other, Farvar had written one and Knelman had written the other. What was to be done? The declaration itself had been neatly typed and reproduced in final form for distribution to the press, but the page which was to contain the population statement had been typed and reproduced in two versions pending the decision of the plenary. The declarations, with alternate page threes, were distributed among the participants, and chairman de Graaf asked each author to read and briefly defend his version of the population statement. There was to be no discussion, but a vote was to be taken between the two, "and then," said de Graaf, "we will see where we go from there."

The vote gave Farvar's version fourteen votes, Knelman's eleven. There was one abstention. De Graaf looked concerned. He hesitated a moment and then declared that the vote was too close to accept a simple majority. Were there any suggestions?

"Mr. Chairman," said Georgescu-Roegen. "I was the first one, at our initial plenary meeting, to propose that we should make a statement about population, which was not in the first work draft." He paused. "I would like to withdraw that proposal." General laughter, applause, whistling in the dark. "I would say that if the establishing of scientific laws is going to be done by majority rule, and the scientists are not able to convince the majority that it is in error on the facts, then there is a kind of dead end, a block that we should avoid simply by removing the bone of contention from the declaration."

There was some confused and desultory discussion. The group could not see how to proceed toward a consensus statement before noon, but no one wished to see the issue dropped either. Chant made a motion for a twenty-minute recess, during which those who agreed with Knelman's version would meet, he said, downstairs.

Eraj objected. "In the spirit in which we have met here we understand that we will give and take here and there. If one scientist differs from another scientist, it should be accepted that we are nevertheless meeting in honest and sincere conscience. This is not the time for lobbying or going about."

Chant countered angrily that his procedural motion was not subject to debate under parliamentary rules. He demanded a ruling from the chairman.

De Graaf allowed the recess, only on the condition that all the delegates remain in the room. Clearly, he agreed with Eraj. Satish Kumar added, "I propose silence and meditation, no more talking."

It was during this recess that Al Hassler pulled from his pocket a third version which he had had the foresight to compose, combining elements of both Farvar's and Knelman's statements (which had themselves already incorporated elements of Mussard's). Hassler's compromise solved the problem of population control by mostly avoiding it. The statement opens with a sentence of Knelman's, which asserts that however it is reached, there is an ineluctable limit to human population size. "It is apparent that human population growth cannot continue indefinitely in a finite environment with finite resources." But all of Knelman's references to programs of population limitation had been deleted. The nearest the compromise came to them was in a sentence of Farvar's: "A true improvement in the living conditions of the people of developing countries would go further in stabilizing population growth than programs of population control." Thus, the compromise neither calls for such programs nor rules them out. But it does state that population cannot grow forever. After the recess it was read, voted on, and adopted in quick order. Nineteen voted for, six against, and still the one abstained. The plenary adjourned, much relieved to Stockholm for the press conference at ABF.

But population hadn't been put to rest. It continued to be the thorniest issue around town. The real climax came on Friday, June ninth, when Paul Ehrlich arrived in Stockholm. People were laying for Ehrlich, whom they had come to see as a Machiavellian architect of imperialism. At lunchtime, he was meeting the press at the Grand Hotel downtown, but he was due to speak at the Environment Forum at one o'clock. When the time came, Elisabeth Wettergren, the hefty, charmingly crazy executive secretary of the Forum, simply marched into the press conference where Ehrlich was besieged and took him by the arm to a waiting car, which drove them to the art school on the outskirts of town where the Environment Forum was encamped. "I promised my friends I'd bring him here," Elisabeth announced in her punchy voice, "and I wouldn't disappoint my friends." It was a coup.

But Elisabeth's coup of roping the day's most controversial figure for the Forum was only the beginning, and even Elisabeth, with her flair for the dramatic, couldn't have foreseen that another coup was hatching even as she spoke —a coup apparently conceived and staged by none other than the ubiquitous (if not insidious) Dr. M. Taghi Farvar of Iran, heading a small but determined band of revolutionaries from assorted third-world lands. This band had its base of operations in OI Committee International, although several of their number were also Dai Dong Conference participants.

The Forum's program was to begin with a press conference of its own, to be followed by a panel discussion on population. One or two questions were asked, and Ehrlich, a man accustomed to public notice, answered them confidently, at ease with his facts, throwing in a lot of baseball metaphors that must have somewhat bewildered the European press—whole-new-ball-games, curves, out-of-the-parks, and so forth. Ehrlich's a professor at a high-class university, but he talks like a regular guy.

Suddenly, there was a flurry at the side of the long speakers' platform. I could see Taghi and Obi Chizea and a few others pushing their way to the platform. Obi passed behind Ehrlich's chair, seized the microphone from the startled chairman, kindly Englishman Peter Scott of the World Wildlife Fund, and announced that the press conference was over, that she was assuming chairmanship of the panel, and that the panel would be enlarged (they weren't throwing Ehrlich out, she insisted) by the addition of third-world people who could add the missing perspective. The Forum's press officer appealed to the audience for support against the unconscionable putsch, announcing bravely that the Forum would not be bullied, that the press conference would go on as scheduled. He demanded to know whether this assault on freedom of the press was to be condoned, but the audience seemed all in favor of the revolution. They cheered and applauded Obi's takeover of the chair and her throaty dismissal of the press, and the press itself was busily and happily enough jotting notes and filming some real action, for a change, instead of just more talk, talk, talk. Obi agreed, actually, to share the chair with Scott, who had behaved like a real gentleman through the whole thing, reasonable, unruffled, and harmless.

Taghi stood behind Obi as she fielded questions and dispensed the floor, and it was difficult not to see him in the role of mustachioed and slightly villainous genius of the show. Those with a better view were able to see that the real genius was Barry Commoner, who had stationed himself on a balcony overlooking the audience at the back of the room from which he was apparently signaling Taghi and his friends, and sending down questions for panelists and members of the audience to put to Ehrlich. Ehrlich suspected as much, although he must not have seen his opponent. At one point he looked around the room and, noting that the putsch was obviously Commoner's show, asked "So where's Barry Baby?" But Barry wasn't saying.

But Obi is tough, and not easily manipulated. Even

Ehrlich was impressed. "Ms. Obi Chizea proved both intelligent and fair," he wrote in his account of the debacle.[8] "It is to her great credit that a little was rescued from what otherwise promised to be a total disaster." It *was* pretty disastrous. Ehrlich bore it creditably, patiently explaining and explaining again his position, never allowing himself to respond in kind to the attacks of other (mostly uninformed) panelists. He explained that he had changed his mind about (and now made public recantation of) his earlier view, expressed in *The Population Bomb,* that industrialized countries like the U.S. should tie foreign aid to programs of population control. But his explanations were ignored by most of the revolutionary panelists. They continued their attacks, often by misquoting and misinterpreting Ehrlich's words. At one point, for example, Ehrlich had said with heavy irony that conservative economists in the West defend imperialist exploitation as a "favor" to third-world countries who depend on sales of their raw materials. A young man from Mexico whom Taghi had introduced as "a doctoral candidate" (which sounds better than "graduate student") missed Ehrlich's irony, apparently didn't listen to the rest of what he said, and took this condescension to be Ehrlich's own position. His attack on that ground dismayed even the partisan audience, from which rose a vapor of low moans. The moans turned to snickers when a young Senegalese took up the attack under the limp banner of the same misapprehension. "There were the familiar accusations of genocide and assertions that redistribution of wealth would automatically result in an end to population growth by means of a demographic transition," wrote Ehrlich. "As usual, the more radical participants were long on rhetoric and short on facts. . . . The sessions were not a complete wasteland of know-nothingism, however," Ehrlich continued. "Dr. Yusuf Ali Eraj from Kenya shocked his doctrinaire cohorts by pointing out that family planning

---

[8] Paul Ehrlich, "A Crying Need for Quiet Conferences," *Science and Public Affairs*, Vol. 28, No. 7 (Sept., 1972), p. 31.

alone would not suffice to bring population growth in under-developed countries under control."[9]

Eraj, though, was with the OI group in charging that the population issue is a political smokescreen. In Kenya there is no difficulty getting foreign-aid money to finance new family-planning measures. There are already more than twenty different family-planning agencies and services. But it is almost impossible to get money to finance a new school. "Does anyone think that girls who have been to school will go on having ten children?" he asked rhetorically. The public is being conditioned, he said, to see population as the major world problem in order to shift the emphasis from the real problems of economic development. But Eraj is himself a family-planning expert. "Family planning is the felt need of mankind. But if family planning does not control the population, for God's sake don't drop it like a hot brick. These people are misguided—some of them have got the wrong motives. They spend a lot of money in a lot of countries to control the population, because somebody has told them that family planning is the way to population control. But the population will not be controlled by family planning. Family planning is basically for the well-being of man. That means that if a woman comes to you and says, 'I just had a baby two months ago, and I want to have another in three years,' you help her, because that is in her interest. But if another comes and says, 'I've been waiting three years and I haven't had a baby,' well, don't turn her away and say, 'That's not my job.'" He pointed out the irony that family-planning measures cannot be instituted even in France and Italy, which are under the domination of the Catholic Church, or even in much of the United States. In nineteenth-century Europe, when people began living and eating better, population growth slowed. "Why should not the same thing happen in the third world?"

The OI takeover of the Environment Forum extended

[9] Ibid., pp. 31–32.

into the evening, when another panel with Ehrlich had been scheduled. This panel was also (though less histrionically) expanded to include young third-world insurgents, including Jurgenne Primavera as chairman. "The low point of the day," wrote Ehrlich of the evening's festivities, "occurred during the evening session (also controlled by the 'Third World' group) when M. Taghi Farvar, a graduate student from Iran, billed as an 'environmental biologist,'[10] presented an incredible child's garden of demography illustrated with eight or 10 badly prepared slides. As the audience drifted off to sleep, Farvar demonstrated that he understood very little about the demographic transition. Hopefully he will take the trouble to learn more before he returns to Iran to help his people."

But there were, as Ehrlich notes, other points of view represented and argued. Fred T. Sai, Ghanaian assistant secretary-general of the International Planned Parenthood Federation, challenged the right of anyone to speak for all of Africa. In general, the OI people claimed to speak not only for all of Africa, but for the rest of the third world, too. Sai insisted that family planning is a necessary part of the "package deal" of development, along with nutrition programs and health care which third-world countries need to break the vicious cycle in which they now are hopelessly spinning. We need to "hook" women on contraception, he said. An American on the panel who had worked in family-planning clinics in India spoke of the population issue from the viewpoint of the individual woman who must bear and care for the children that happen. He cited the hundreds of women who had come to his clinic—eighteen-, twenty-year-old women in their sixth and seventh pregnancies, who wanted desperately not to have to bear more children, but were utterly ignorant of ways to prevent it. He lamented the depersonalized politicization of the population issue, which works to keep birth-control information from women who want it. These women cannot control their own lives, but are trapped in the cycle of bearing and raising children.

[10] Farvar holds a Ph.D. in biology from Washington University.

Jurgenne Primavera took the privilege of the chair at this point to bear witness of the individual woman's point of view. She had been "hooked," she said, on contraception. For five years she and her husband were childless because of what she discovered to be the insidious influence of Western imperialist thought. She has returned to her people, she told us, and to her native culture, and she has shed these foreign ideas, and contraception with them. She was proud to report that she has added to the population of the Philippines.

"The OI group is a very open group. I have found nobody restricting me from talking about whatever I thought was right," Dr. Eraj told me a few days later. "If they had not taken over that day, a very different picture would have been given to the world. After all, the world at the moment is looking to Stockholm. That day they didn't stop Paul Ehrlich from saying anything. But he didn't have the monopoly of the panel. And he did admit where he had gone wrong."

Dai Dong Deputy Director Jens Brøndum was also sympathetic. "The problem is that the OI group is so new and so eager to clarify their own identity that they are very wary of direct cooperation with anybody else, quite simply. And there is something right in their viewpoint. They want to see everything excusively from the basis of the third world, because they say it has never been done. You are always seeing it from the first world. And I respect that. We have suppressed in an intellectually imperialistic way the third-world viewpoint every time. So I understand it. Their tactical problem is that if they don't very soon affiliate with progressive scientists and activists in the Western world, I don't see how they can change anything in the Western countries where all their analysis points out the changes must take place. They can attract strong allies by seeing everything from the point of view of the third world, but the final result they're looking for is that something be changed in the first world. And they cannot accomplish that if they don't find a way of affiliating strongly with us and others who'll help them change things."

Others were less charitable. Fred Knelman, who had thrashed through the population issue with Farvar that frustrating Monday night before the press conference, spoke bitterly. "I object very fundamentally to the idea of taking over an organization, of diverting them or manipulating them for one's own political purposes. I believe this is an improper tactic, and ends up as a self-defeating tactic. And I have the very strong sense that, without naming names, this attempt was made. My position was not one of ideological opposition to these people, but of tactical opposition. I felt that they would split the conference if they persisted with their tactics, and that they were not ready for anything but unconditional acceptance of their position. They weren't ready for a compromise, and the other side—the people who are basically either politically neutral or politically conservative—in effect said to me, if this conference, called as an environmental conference based on the Menton Statement, is in some way subverted by a small group who are simply using it for their own ideological ends, then we will not sign the declaration and we will walk out. . . . You can't have it both ways. You can't subscribe to Dai Dong, you can't come to Dai Dong to subvert it to something it's not, or to its opposite."

Even before the population issue had been settled, Henry Regier had voiced similar feelings. "The revolutionaries here—at least the chief revolutionary, if I recognize him—can't lose. If the thing breaks apart, he can rationalize by saying, well, it wasn't any good anyway. If he can get as much of his revolutionary jargon in here as possible, he wins that way. So I suspect his strategy is, if it doesn't go the way I like, I'll try to destroy it. Well, the environmentalists' strategy can be exactly the same, because if it is polarized any further, there'll be so little environmental interest in here that we can pull out and say, ah, the whole damned thing was polarized by a couple of forces long in existence, which haven't given the new force any chance at all."

Regier explained what he sees as the inherent contradiction between the political analysis of the OI group and the fundamental insight of ecology that the world is an inextricably interrelated system. "They have to cease being so very religious about their Marxism. There's no practicing Marxist in any position of authority that is half so dogmatic and doctrinaire as these revolutionaries living in North America. They talk with such a very puritanical, categorical sort of way, very simplistic. You know, *sin, truth, error* . . . They argue a systems approach, and then argue categories, dichotomies, *good, evil*, and cause-and-effect chains. And the two are incompatible. You can't think categories, dichotomies, *good, evil*, and cause-and-effect chains, and at the same time say, here's a system running and it all hangs together. The two are alternative ways of looking at things. And they're very importantly alternative. And the ecological way is the way that says, the *system*, and says, it docsn't do much good at this stage to find out who happens to be the chief ogre. Because if you kill the chief ogre, another chief ogre of essentially the same kind is going to take his place."

Conrad Istock viewed OI's tactics in the larger context of their real, long-range goals. "Their militancy implies that they have a program. And they don't. They don't really have a program for any nation they represent (or any other one) to get out of its present difficulties. It's people like Eraj, in the intermediate position, who hold out much more hope. Because people will keep talking to him. He's not telling them to turn off the green revolution or forget their first oil refinery. He's telling them basically what they can hope to accomplish *after* they do the minimal amount for the population. To me that's much more revolutionary. He's taking nations that in many cases have a vicious economic stratification, and telling them, we're going to get rid of this, you know; we're going to do something about it. But he's still more likely to be listened to, unless he cracks up under the strain. And Obi Chizea has many of the same qualities. She was always standing on the fence, to a great extent, trying to talk about nonpolitical things that can be done for people in a nonpolitical vein. Taghi's militancy is something he learned in the United States, I'm afraid. Every disenchanted American student behaves like that, and the response is pretty much uniformly the same from the establishment. Actually, many of the more effective activist students have adopted different tactics. His tactics are much more like those of the sixties."

The Dai Dong Declaration was presented publicly to a jam-packed press conference at the ABF House on Tuesday. In the evening, the participants returned to Graninge for a final plenary meeting to work out plans for the promised appendices of specific proposals for action. It wasn't clear how to proceed, however, particularly in light of the difficulty of reaching consensus just on the declaration of principles. How could the group now in one evening agree on a set of concrete recommendations? Someone urged that proposals would be the "flesh and blood" of the abstract principles enunciated in the declaration. But another saw no hope of coming to agreement, and felt that the proposals should be deferred to another forum. "These ideas are not doomed eternally," he said. It was decided (once again) to hand the knot of proposals already written up for workgroup sessions to Dorothy Maas, who with the help of several volunteers would see if she could find some order among the strands. She couldn't. The committee met the next day and decided very quietly, without calling a press conference to announce the fact, to put all the valuable recommendations into a box, to wrap the box carefully, and to send it to the Nyack headquarters of Dai Dong. And then the committee decided to have a drink.

V

Declaring

For the Dai Dong Conference there was a lull till Thursday evening when Al Hassler was scheduled to read the Dai Dong Declaration before the plenary session of UNCHE, which had been under way since the beginning of the week. Since I'd come to Stockholm with the intention of covering UNCHE's proceedings as well as everybody else's (UNCHE was, after all, everybody else's point of departure), and I was an accredited correspondent with a badge and one of those embossed portfolios and all, I got myself over to the Old Parliament Building the first free day (which happened to be Wednesday) to see how things were going.

Dull, is how. I'd been warned they would be. I'd been warned by people who knew that the last place in Stockholm I'd want to hang around was the U.N. But I felt I ought to be conscientious, first of all, and secondly I know that even dullness can have its rewards. For instance, I actually enjoy sitting a whole day or two in the still air of a library, pinning down (say) a glancing reference to the minor commentary of an obscure and saintly exegete in a book that leaves its rusty, crumbling leather on my fingers. It's satisfying, like marking off the first five hundred years in purgatory. Or struggling with a Latin sentence, staring at the jumble of words with a blank look, until the jumble suddenly resolves itself and meaning magically appears. But the meetings of UNCHE were dull beyond meaning, beyond redemption. Dull to make your joints ache as if with fever, to make you feel the joy of playing hookey when you quietly rose, begged pardon of the dutiful condemned who remained in the gallery pews, and in as dignified a manner as it was possible to bring off (so as to suggest a pressing engagement) fled.

It's not that what UNCHE accomplished is dull. Quite the contrary. Or how they accomplished it. But the meetings themselves were so pat, so cut-and-dried, so lacking the faintest spark of spontaneity! Whatever went on in the public sessions had been so thoroughly worked out beforehand in private that each delegation knew not only what it was going to say, but also what the others would reply. And the delegates are bad actors, who often seem as bored with the necessity of going through the motions as, in consequence, the audience becomes watching them.

Actually, the thing was seductive for the first few minutes. The chambers of the Old Parliament were quite magnificent with their glossy oak paneling and desks and galleries, their plush seats rich as putting greens. You looked down from the press gallery on the assembled distinguished representatives from more countries than you could shake a stick at, sitting neatly, alphabetically in rows, the colors of their clothes bright and crisp in the television lights—brown men, black men, pink men, yellow men, pale greenish men, men with paunches and with bald spots, skinny men, men with curly hair, nappy hair, straight blond hair, some wearing caps, and several women in elegant, bright-colored dresses. Everybody civil (if not smiling) and dignified, coming together, now, once and for all to rid the air and water of this unpleasantness we're all so concerned about. You could look down on these men and women, earnestly speaking on behalf of their governments (if not of their people), earnestly appearing to listen to each other, taking the world's business into their hands and taking care of it, responsibly doing their jobs—you could look down on this gleaming spectacle and quite (for a moment) forget what people were actually (at that moment) perpetrating on each other in the world.

Jean Mussard had explained to the Dai Dong Conference why the proceedings of the U.N., if you regard them as a debate, are so dull. Someone had complained that the U.N. cannot hope to rise to the present needs of the world because a bureaucracy is inherently slow and unresponsive to public pressure. "Since we speak about the U.N.," replied Mussard, "and I happen to have been a bureaucrat there—the real problem is not that the U.N. works slowly and is not that they are bureaucrats. There are very good people there. The real problem is first of all that what we call a discussion never can take place in the U.N., and you can't blame anybody for this. It's the system which cannot produce a discussion, for a very simple reason. In a meeting—let's take for example the preparatory committee of the Stockholm Conference—you have around the table about the same number of people we have here, but they are all governmental delegates with briefs. We also use the word 'discussion' in the U.N., but it has quite a different meaning. What is called a 'discussion' in the U.N. is an exchange of briefs. The Englishman will say, 'My government will agree to this, and will not agree to that.' He cannot say more than that. And he can listen to the French delegate saying, 'My government wants this, and is unalterably opposed to that.' But it's the *system*, not the human beings who take part in it. The other reason it doesn't work (it's not a question of working slowly; it doesn't work at all in certain areas) is that certain subjects are taboo. There are certain issues which simply cannot be raised in the U.N., and these are the issues which touch upon the interests of the established political and economic structure. These subjects are well known, and what is called 'work' whenever they are being dealt with consists simply in producing papers to confuse the issues. It is impossible to do anything different because this also is part of the system. So I don't think it's worthwhile criticizing the U.N. in general terms. What is important is to see why in certain cases it may work and in other cases it may not. This is a structural question."

Mussard had reason to know the structure of the United Nations, and more particularly of UNCHE, because

he had been hired—even before Maurice Strong was
named secretary-general—as director of the secretariat of
the Stockholm conference. Several months later Strong
joined the secretariat, and tactical differences arose between
the two that led to Mussard's firing. Mussard saw the hand-
writing on the wall when Strong asked him privately not to
present a report he had prepared for the preparatory committee on the ground that the report was too radical. It was
not, Mussard feels, that Strong disagreed with him philosoph-
ically or ideologically, but that he was convinced the governments would reject the report's recommendations. Strong's
diplomacy in this instance was a part of what Mussard
described later as the "self-censorship of the secretariat."
His own view of the secretariat's role—a view responsible in
part for his dismissal—was that it should provide leadership
that would in effect stretch the natural inclinations of governments to pursue only their parochial self-interest. "We
know, we accept it as a fact of life, that the U.N. cannot do
what it wants because the U.N. is simply an organization of
governments. O.K. But even given this fact, the U.N. is an
organization with its own status, its own staff, its own general secretary, its own responsibilities towards the governments. And it is part of these responsibilities that the U.N.
take the intellectual and moral responsibility for what it
proposes to the member states. Whether they accept it or
reject it or accept only part of it—this is the member states'
affair. But the U.N. has responsibility for what it proposes.
And this is not pure philosophy. This means, for example,
that in preparing the declaration for this conference (which
was supposed to be an inspiring document, and on which
many hopes were built), the U.N. should have taken full
responsibility, moral and intellectual. It should have prepared the draft itself—together with all sorts of people, if
you like—but the secretary-general should have been solely
responsible for calling upon this or that man, philosopher,
scientist, or whomever (and he should even have taken the
pains to think about it himself), for using the knowledge of
his own staff (who know much more than what is said in that
draft declaration), and for drawing up a draft to show to the

member states. Then, of course, they would have discussed it, and deleted some parts of it, and changed others. But instead of doing that, it was decided formally in February, 1971, to set up a committee of representative governments to prepare the draft. And this is what I mean by self-censorship. This is pure nonsense. This is submitting to the governments a draft which they have prepared themselves. It is called a U.N. draft, but it isn't. It's not a U.N. draft. The U.N. has simply done the editing, the translations, and the circulations. There were plenty of people in the system, including myself, who were prepared to take full responsibility; the Secretary-General was legally entitled, in fact he was even *asked* to do it. These are the normal rules of the game. The Secretary-General proposes something, and the governments accept this or that part of his proposals. And then the public can compare; you know where you are and what is still to be done and so on. But if the U.N. never opens its mouth, never puts anything on paper before it knows how the governments will react, or if it actually asks the governments to do its own job in order to be sure it won't say anything they might not like, then the U.N. could just as well disappear. It's just fooling the people, telling them that the U.N. does something. It does paper work—that's all, in this case. If you read carefully the constitution and the staff statutes you will see for example that there is an oath—when I came to New York I was asked to take an oath that I would never accept any instructions from any government. Which is very nice. You've barely taken the oath and already you're taking instructions. And if you don't, people look at you as if you were an idiot, or a madman, and you are in trouble. So why don't we at least play the legal game? We have the right to do that. We are being *asked* to do that. It's on paper."

A fabulous character called Maurice String appeared in several stories in the daily newspaper produced by Environment Forum. The cut-and-dried dullness of UNCHE sessions was captured in this "scoop":

Our Eco-correspondent has now got the first news of a new String Plan to speed up the plenary sessions of

UNCHE. In future, String hopes, speeches will sound like this:

"Mr. Chairman, Distinguished Delegates. Number 1, Number 3, Number 7, Nos. 8 to 11 inclusive, number 34, and above all number 43 . . ." (Applause)

Interpreted according to String's Pocket Guide for Delegates, this reads:

No. 1: "My delegation wishes to thank the Secretary-General and his staff for the magnificent work they have done in preparing this Conference."

No. 7: "My country has a special interest in preserving a human environment in which all our citizens can achieve the fullest development of their economic, social and cultural potential."

No. 10: "My government is currently preparing a comprehensive national plan for the protection of the physical and natural environment."

No. 34: "We wish to express our wholehearted support for the passage in the Draft Declaration which emphasizes the need to guarantee national sovereignty in matters of environmental policy."

No. 43: "My country faces overwhelming problems of economic development. We could not be party to any recommendations from this Conference which did not guarantee compensation for any loss of trade resulting from measures taken nationally or internationally, to protect the environment."

So Wednesday I spent hanging around UNCHE, drifting in and out of committee sessions, trying very hard to concentrate on what was being argued and counterargued—really putting my whole mind to it, without much luck. But it was different that evening. The city of Stockholm gave a reception for delegates and correspondents in the courtyard of the town hall, engraved invitations to which had been included in the vinyl portfolio. Stockholm's famous town hall is a huge brick monolith, a square tower rising at one corner, topped with a suddenly ornate cupola. It is a severe, oddly charming building surrounding a paved court, the flat brick of the far wall opening in a series of low roman arches which give onto an outer grass courtyard, directly on the water of Lake Mälar. A few statues and pools around the garden make a gesture toward elegance, but there is nothing lavish about the place. Lutheranism indulging a bit stiffly, with an awkward smile, in the pleasures of culture.

But although the seat of the city government's daily business wasn't lavish, Stockholm's reception for its global guests was. Dozens of long, white-decked tables were set around the lawn of the outer court, laden to groaning with pickled herring, fried herring, herring sodden in wine and in mustard sauce, smoked salmon, baked salmon, meatballs, sliced roast beef and sausage, a variety of sauces, half a dozen different salads, as many cheeses, and an assortment of rolls and bread. Elderly ladies in peasant costumes strolled about offering wine, or grape juice masquerading as wine (for the abstemious), or beer. In the inner court, a military band played for arriving guests. A sailboat race was in progress just off the water's edge; a genial young Swede in a blazer conscientiously announced the positions of the boats, and finally the winners, over a loudspeaker, although (not unlike the regular sessions of UNCHE) none of the guests were paying the slightest attention. He was just able to elicit a scattered rattle of applause from the dozen or so guests who happened to notice as he grandly crowned some pretty young Swedish thing Queen of Lake Mälar. She smiled bravely and the delegates went on swallowing herring.

Frankly, the affair was a disappointment. I'd eaten an extremely plain dinner out at Graninge, thinking the reception would be mostly for drinking. I was completely prepared to get honestly sloshed on Swedish schnapps, of which there wasn't a drop (although Swedes aren't normally Lutheran about their booze). Instead, all this elegant, seductive food, with which I further and obscenely stuffed myself, so as not to miss out on anything free. Like Stockholm's vinyl portfolio, this alimentary extravaganza fairly clobbered one over the head with its ironies in the context of UNCHE, gathered to worry among other apocalyptic horrors over the chronic hunger of fully half of humanity. Confronted by an interviewer on this point, one elegant British lady replied unabashedly between bites, "This is a conference on the environment, not on salvation." And certainly we all went away gratefully convinced of the geniality and largess of our hosts.

The next afternoon, Al Hassler was to read the Dai Dong Declaration to the U.N. I arrived early at the "People's House," the large, trade unions' auditorium where UNCHE's plenary sessions were held, and found Al coolly sipping a gin and tonic in the lobby. A number of speakers had been stuck into the agenda ahead of him, so there would be an hour or more to wait. I sat with him for a few minutes, drank a beer from a paper cup, and then poked my head into the meeting. The assembly hall was different from the stately Old Parliament Building—thoroughly modern, clean, efficient, cold. The clear, white lights of the television crews made the proceedings look embedded in Lucite. Someone stood at the podium reading a speech. Behind a long desk across the dais sat Maurice Strong, Ingmund Bengtsson, president of the plenary, and four or five other UNCHE officials, each with a placard in front of him indicating his function. They appeared to be listening; Strong, with his earphones on, head cocked attentively to one side, was half turned in his chair to the speaker. From time to time, messages would come from behind the dais to one of the officials, and there would be a swiveling of chairs, whisperings back and forth, significant glances, and occasionally important goings out and comings in, the speaker at the podium droning on, all this time, relentless.

I looked down on the half-empty hall with a sinking feeling. Dai Dong had seriously hoped to sock it to UNCHE with a forthright, hard-hitting declaration that would rouse the stodgy politicians. Now it looked as though the forthright declaration would just be swallowed, among hundreds of other papers arguing this position or that, like so much plankton down the maw of a whale. I went to the lobby, where certainly no less could be happening than in the plenary, and possibly considerably more. Not much going on there either. Delegates chatted here and there, or read a newspaper, or wrote letters; reporters milled. I spotted a Chinese delegate in his blue uniform relaxing on a sofa, and since everyone had been saying for the last few days that the Chinese were the key to everything, and that you weren't going to get the real story if you didn't talk to *them*, I determined to use any pretext at all to get the real story. I took a seat next to him, casually pretending to look through some papers for a while, then turned and brazenly struck up an inane conversation. What did he "think of" the conference? Was he enjoying himself in Stockholm? (He was a member of the embassy staff, permanently in Stockholm.) Had he heard of the Dai Dong Independent Conference? "No," he said, smiling pleasantly. Had he heard of Dai Dong? He gave me a blank look. It's Chinese, I explained, and showed him a brochure on which the characters were printed. He glanced at it, then looked up at me and smiled. "Dha t'ong," he said, condescendingly correcting my pronunciation. I explained about the Independent Conference, and he nodded and smiled.

He was affable, talkative even, but classically inscrutable. Whenever I tried to make the move from pleasantry to real question—What did he think about East Germany's exclusion from UNCHE? Was China pursuing public measures of population control? Should the present environmental conference have taken up the issue of ecocide?—he smilingly but firmly put me off. China's positions on these questions were perfectly clear and had been articulated adequately in her various papers and speeches. It would be pointless, he told me, for him to try to amplify on these points—a conversation stopper that taxed my powers to get even the pleasantries going again with some fresh *non sequitur* or banality. Meanwhile, a small cluster of reporters and photographers had gathered vulture-like around us (figuring I guess that I was getting the fabulous real story which resided with the Chinese) taking pictures and straining to hear what wasn't being said.

Al was still waiting to go on when I finished my abortive journey to the East, and was working on another gin and tonic as the speeches dragged on inside the hall. What we could not know was that a drama was unfolding inside the plenary (even—ironically—as I was pumping my Chinese delegate) staged by the Chinese themselves. Unexpectedly (except to the United States and other major powers, who had, according to *The New York Times*, worked frantically "behind the scenes" to prevent it) the Chinese had asked for the floor and had been granted precedence over scheduled speeches to propose that the draft declaration, prepared by the 27-nation preparatory committee in over a year of work, be submitted for revision to a new committee comprising all 113 nations represented at Stockholm. It had been assumed that the draft would be accepted by the conference as a formality with little or no discussion in the closing hours of the two weeks of UNCHE. But Tang Ke, leader of his delegation, argued that China, which had joined the U.N. in October, 1971, had not been able to participate in the formulation of the draft, nor had many other third-world nations. There was a momentary flurry of confusion in the plenary hall, then an hour and a half of courteous debate, mostly in support of the resolution. The U.S. and Canada voiced "reservations," but felt, in the end, obliged to join in the unanimous approval of the Chinese resolution.

Here was an unexpected parallel between the Dai Dong and United Nations declarations. Both documents, prepared and submitted as drafts to their respective conferences, were thrown open to drastic revision, albeit for divergent reasons. It might be said that the Dai Dong staff avoided the "self-censorship" of which Mussard accused the U.N. Secretariat and exercised the kind of moral leadership he was insisting on in writing the draft it felt the situation required. It did not consult widely on the acceptability of the draft, and thus the document was not subject to the kind of watering down that often attends everybody's having a shot at the thing. As a result, however, the Dai Dong draft ran into trouble with the delegates, for whom some of the language was too strong, and some not strong enough.

The U.N. Secretariat took an opposite course. It had the member governments themselves prepare the draft, thinking to assure acceptability, if not perfection. Yet the U.N. draft ran into trouble too, because *not all* the member governments, especially China's, had taken part in preparing it. In the end, UNCHE's declaration wasn't as drastically revised as China's procedural victory threatened. Like a great deal else about UNCHE, the revision was largely a gesture, but a gesture not without meaning. No one, it turned out, had sufficiently taken account of third-world frustrations and aspirations. This had been as true for Dai Dong as it was for the U.N. One way or another, the third-world countries were going to make themselves felt at Stockholm. And they did, in more ways than just one.

The vote on the Chinese resolution had been taken, and the delegates began packing and closing their briefcases and leaving the hall for dinner. To my relief—as I contemplated Al's addressing not just a perfunctory audience, but a nonexistent one—Strong sent out a message that the entire agenda, including the reading of the Independent Declaration, would be tabled until tomorrow afternoon's session. So we packed our own briefcases and departed for dinner, too.

The turn of events somewhat undercut Dai Dong's scheduled program for the evening. A main exhibition hall in Stockholm's Museum of Modern Art had been hired for a panel discussion of Dai Dong's Independent Declaration and UNCHE's Draft Declaration on the Human Environment, which China had just succeeded in reopening to major revision. The idea had been to get a representative or two from UNCHE to debate representatives of the Dai Dong Conference. Whether it was the last-minute confusion over the Chinese move (as Strong claimed), or simply reluctance to confront criticism in public, no delegate was available for the program, and Strong sent Barbara Ward (Lady Jackson), the well-known economist who had collaborated with René Dubos in writing the more-or-less official book for the Stockholm conference, *Only One Earth*, and Walter Hickel, renegade U.S. Secretary of the Interior in the first years of the Nixon administration, to speak for UNCHE. With them on the platform, incongruously surrounded by huge, brilliantly colored canvases and sculptures—the colors

and the white walls intensified by television lights—were
Dai Dong's Mussard, Istock, Eraj, and Obi Chizea.

Barbara Ward confronted the lights through a pair of
sunglasses that made her look like a celebrity, not a lady
economist. She opened the program with a few general
remarks based on her personal observations of poverty in
the world. She spoke poignantly of "children of ten with
anemia, which is incurable because their diet is bad; babies
of a year suffering from protein deficiency, which means that
their brains will never in fact be fully human, because you
cannot educate a mind that has not been able to grow in the
first place. And it seemed to me," she said, "that the contrast between the inability of the very rich to do anything,
and the deepening, deepening problems of the environment
of the destitute poor, is the *real* limit on our planet." She
was alluding, of course, to the efforts currently being made
to determine the limits to growth of our finite global system.
"You can plot as much as you like that we'll run out of
resources by the year 2050 or 3000. My friends, I don't
think we'll get there unless we somehow reverse the inordinate and appalling and widening gap between rich and
poor. . . . In all questions of resources, of environment, all
questions of whom we save and whom we don't save, my
priority is for that third of the human race that may not even
reach full human stature because of their devastating
poverty."

Barbara Ward offered no direct comparison of the two
declarations, but she did make a critique of Dai Dong's
on its own terms. "First of all, if you're making a declaration, what do you want to do with it? Do you want governments to listen, or public opinion? I imagine that the declaration you're making is for public opinion. If I may say so,
Mrs. Smith, going down to the supermarket, isn't going to
read it, chums. And she's the one who in fact is going to go
on wanting all these splendid consumer goods that are going
to destroy the universe." It was a question of language, she
was saying. "If you are going to have a declaration for the
voter, the people who put the governments in power, there
must be some greater simplicity of language, something that

tells the ordinary citizen, 'Watch out, chum—it's going to hit *you*.' "

Yes, it was a question of language. The struggle to produce a declaration had been mostly a question of language, not just because a declaration is only words anyway, but because the motives, the goals, the vision behind the words were not the crux of the dispute. The problem of third-world perspective, for instance, resolved itself largely to a question of language. The mostly Western scientists—all with the best of intentions, feeling themselves in solidarity with the deprived people of the third world as well as the first and second—strained to express themselves unambiguously, precisely, as they have been trained, as scientists, to do. Yet for all its precision, their message, it was argued, would be misconstrued in the third world; radicals there would see precise scientific formulations of environmental problems as a mask to justify continued exploitation of their people. The language that means one thing to the Western scientist means something else in the third world.

"In environmental problems," Chilean Jaime Hurtubia had told me, "the most important thing is to capture the trust of the developing countries. The natural environment of the third world, our resources, our tropical forests with their natural production of oxygen, is the key to the world of the future, something that all the world will need tomorrow very much." To obtain the trust of the people of the third world, he had said, the Dai Dong Declaration needed to speak in the language of identification with their problems and their aspirations, not in the language of scientific nicety. Dai Dong must risk being misunderstood by the scientific establishment, because the solution to the global crisis does not depend on the establishment in the West, but on the people of the developing countries. In effect the argument calls for a kind of self-censorship different from the U.N.'s (to which Mussard objected), yet ironically parallel to it. There are taboos. Certain things can't be said; certain language can't be used—not because it isn't true, scientifically, but because it is politically offensive to certain people one can no longer afford to offend.

Austrian Ernst Winter expressed a similar reservation. "It's paternalistic, you see. We are speaking to them, we are giving them advice—how it should be done and what will happen—instead of identifying with them. I think the language of identification, the language of sensitivity, may be much less precise than the one which we've used, but to me it is better than a precise scientific language which is at best the didactic language of a bunch of wise people who know everything better. And this is a weakness, not only of this group's approach, but of the approach of many well-meaning groups."

At the modern museum, however, Conrad Istock took up the challenge of Barbara Ward's criticism of the Independent Declaration. "It would have been a mistake to write it for Mrs. Smith. We wrote it for scientists and intellectuals and policy-makers. It's quite a wide group. . . . At this point, trying to explain to Mrs. Smith why we need redistribution of wealth and resources, political influence, and that sort of thing is worthless—it's a waste of time to try. We're in the business of explaining it to ourselves at this point, and that's the value of the Dai Dong document. And we did a pretty good job of explaining it to ourselves and putting it down on paper." Dai Dong's purpose, he went on, was to formulate an analysis free (as free as possible) of ideology and political allegiance, with the ultimate goal of equalizing the conditions of living for all people. He spoke of the continuing struggle between scientific knowledge and political power. "At no time in the past has the world as a whole tried to impose so much ideology on the science of biology. We have the really astounding periods, for example, in the trials and tribulations of Galileo, or the fate of the geneticists under Lysenkoism in the U.S.S.R. But I think in *every* country today there is an attempt, by *every* nation's government, to obscure the facts and principles of ecology in order to defend very ancient and diverse national traditions."

Istock spoke of the absurdity, in the humbling context of billions of years of global history, of defending as if they were absolute the concept of the nation state and the various ideologies on which it claims to be based. The space their existence would occupy on a time scale of the earth's history is no more than a pin prick's width. "The basic processes in the world will always be transactions in energy and matter. This is the proper subject matter of ecology. The recent economic history of man is pretty well summed up as an attempt to alter and convert to seemingly beneficial uses these transactions of matter and energy. Matter and energy remain and will remain the sources of economic wealth, no matter how abstract economics becomes. It is not simply a game of life played by economists and politicians. There is at least one more player at the table, and that is nature. And nature," Istock concluded by warning, "is going to play a very hard game indeed."

Walter Hickel spoke next. The problems of managing our household earth, he said, really come down to developing a sense of responsibility for the commons—for air, water, and natural resources. We should put our faith in the United Nations as the vehicle for developing that sense of responsibility, he urged. And we should have faith that the technology that has caused the environmental crisis will also be able to solve it. He did not foresee doomsday, he said hopefully. But for all his good intentions and hopefulness, Hickel (and others who trust in technology to save us) missed the point that it is not technology, but the people who have created and who guide the technology that are responsible for the environmental crisis. And while it is certainly true that technology, even today, *could* solve the problems of pollution and resource depletion, it is not at all clear that *people* can bring themselves to employ technology to that end.

Dr. Eraj noted that the U.N. Draft Declaration, in contradistinction to Dai Dong's, did not place responsibility for environmental degradation on the growing centralization of power and technology, nor did it call for the redistribution of wealth, nor did it criticize the existing systems out of which environmental problems flow, nor did it confront the issue of population. Dai Dong's Independent Declaration, he said, gave UNCHE a lead to follow in redrafting its own declaration now that the draft had been reopened by the Chinese for revision.

Eraj's comments echoed what Fred Knelman had told me the day before. "I read the U.N. declaration vary carefully. And there are points of very significant difference. They're important. I think the U.N. declaration in effect underwrites the idea that although there are some disbenefits from Western technology, basically it has brought more benefits than disbenefits, and basically this is what the third world needs, and basically the classical or traditional economic growth is the answer to the problems of distribution, and so on. We need more economic development so that we can get rid of poverty, and so on. And they do not accept our basic criticism that it's just the reverse—that's not the answer at all. Dai Dong is saying that our present systems are suicidal and will self-destruct."

From his special perspective as someone who has worked within the system of the United Nations, Jean Mussard tried to get at the difference in terms of the organizational structures that produced the two documents. On the one hand you have the predictability, the self-censorship of the UNCHE Secretariat. On the other, you have the openness of Dai Dong. "The United Nations is an organization where one very often can guess one year in advance, or even more, what is or is not going to happen. Dai Dong is the sort of organization where you never know what will happen in the next thirty minutes. This is not necessarily an advantage. It simply shows the difference in structure." Dai Dong's declaration, he said, "is more human, in a way. It's certainly less cautious. People sometimes get quite passionate in the discussion of these issues, and we had that in our own meeting a few days ago. We remained friends, of course, and we agreed finally on a certain text. But if you read it carefully, you will perhaps perceive that it was sometimes difficult to draft it."

To some extent, though, the comparison with UNCHE's document is misleading. For Dai Dong, "Stockholm was a pretext. It was a pretext for trying to put on paper some sort of declaration, some sort of formulation of the problems. And the declaration has its own intrinsic value quite independent of the Stockholm conference. I would say we should have tried to make such a declaration anyway, even if there had been no official Stockholm conference." The difficulties in drafting the declaration arose primarily out of the nature of the pretext itself, the pressure of time. What the declaration really represents is a phase in an ongoing examination of the issues, an ongoing debate. "In real life there are no deadlines—it is a continuing process."

It was late in the evening. It had been a long day. The white lights, the white walls with canvases like windows on a brilliant, crazy landscape, the web of black electrical cables running over the floor in the darkness behind the light, the talk about talk about declarations, in fact the whole week and a half of talk and declaration and ceremony was all spinning itself into wispy threads thinner and thinner in my head. I picked up my briefcase and my camera and the trombone case I'd surreptitiously stuck in a corner of the gallery, snuck out ahead of everybody else, and went to the old town to meet some jazz-musician friends who were playing at a club. Its ancient vaulted brick walls were so packed with sweating, beer-swilling young Swedes that I couldn't get near the bandstand at first. I made myself skinny against a wall, and stood drinking a mug of cold beer, listening to the music and the easy babble of voices. When I'd finished the beer, I slipped around to the side door and rang the bell. A suspicious cook stuck his head out the door, and only hesitantly let me in when I told him I'd been invited to play. People had looked incredulous and snickered when I arrived in Stockholm juggling the absurd trombone case together with suitcase, briefcase, tape recorder, and camera. But the trombone turned out to be as essential as any of them.

It was an instrument of reality in the headiness, the giddiness of the conference and its independent environment. Playing that jazz, feeling the music ride the wave of rhythm, watching the dancers move with the wave who had nothing whatever to say about sewage disposal or chemical fertilizer or methods of population control—who for the moment had only something inconsequential to say to each other, with a gesture—kept me in touch with a world outside the talk. I would come up like a miner from the smoky cellars at two or three in the morning into midsummer daylight and walk in the cool air, listening to the crazy warble of the Nordic birds. Sensible people were at peace in their beds. I was out of my bed, carrying a trombone through the oddly deserted streets of the city—a passage out again into open waters from the insular conferences, to a sense of the wide, living environment all these folks had come to preserve.

Al read the declaration next morning to a sparse plenary. As we were waiting for him to go on, I noticed a small, slowly moving flurry of press around someone serene, obviously important. One of the reporters told me it was Prince Bernhardt of the Netherlands, who had just addressed the conference. When the flurry reached the door and dissipated as the prince stepped into his waiting, appropriately dark limousine, I struck up a conversation with a reporter from Swedish Radio who was gathering taped material for SR's French-language broadcasts. She was delighted to have captured on her tape recorder one princely sentence in French about the urgent need to preserve the environment. Quite a coup. I noticed Arthur Godfrey, his wrinkled, sagging face propped on the crisp, white collar of his shirt, his dark suit set off with a dewy white boutonniere. He stood chatting with equally crisp Russell Train, also, I presume, about the urgent need to preserve the environment.

I went into the plenary hall to listen to Al. He was announced by president Bengtsson. I watched from the press gallery above as he made his way down one of the aisles, then mounted the rostrum. Placing the pages of the declaration on the lectern before him, he started to read. When he finished the delegates applauded politely. And that was that.

VI

Going Home

One didn't realize it immediately, of course. No ceremony marked the occasion. It came over one gradually. One chatted with others who also had been here two weeks, since the beginning of the Dai Dong Conference, and discovered they felt it too. We were only halfway through UNCHE—still a week of talk to go. But the Stockholm adventure had peaked. One still went dutifully through the newspapers and the conference dailies and checked the bulletin boards each morning to find out what was going on. One still spent each day frenziedly rushing in and out of buses, down into the subways and up again, always flashing the free pass, walking, walking miles from one conference center clear across town to another—from the Old Parliament Building over to the New Parliament building, across town to the Grand Hotel, out to the Environment Forum on the outskirts of town, back in to ABF. One still looked wherever one went for the real action, hoped it still was to come, knew reluctantly that something crucial, finally, hadn't happened. Wistfully, one hoped the Hog Farm would still come across with something splashy and beautiful, or that the Chinese were cooking up something sensational behind the closed doors of that committee to revise UNCHE's declaration, or that People's Forum would march in and take over the U.N., or that there would be the monster demonstration and the monster bust the cops had been waiting for, or something, anything. But actually one knew that things were running down.

Stockholm, it has to be said, was a carnival. For all the seriousness of the environmental crisis, the serious intentions of the people who'd come to fix it, the serious talk, and the real accomplishments of both official and unofficial conferences, the atmosphere people were breathing (automobile exhaust aside) was the atmosphere of carnival, of magic, of wishing. And there is only so long you can maintain the mood of carnival. Carnival is always followed by Lent. This is not to denigrate what happened in Stockholm. Not in the least. Humanity would die out without carnival. Without carnival there would be no Lent. Without magic nothing would change. Without wishing there would be no hope. But we knew that the wonderful carnival was just entropically running down.

As it happened, the Hog Farm did come across with something splashy and beautiful, two days before UNCHE shut down: a great open-air fest, an antitype of Stockholm's lavish reception, held in the largest public square in town. Everybody was invited to the Celebration of Life, and nearly everybody came. It began with a chaotic parade of thousands of happy, hippy people, many in costume, with masks on, some with their faces garishly painted. A girl playing a silver flute was followed by a man beating a drum slung over ragged overalls, his hair tied in a bandanna, face painted weirdly white. People kissed and joked and made a fuss over the babies and children in the crowd. The motley parade ended incongruously at gleaming Sergel's Square, the new complex of glass and steel high-rises surrounding an enormous, low, shimmering fountain that looks, in that setting, in that intense June sunlight, not so much like water as itself a cold construction of glass and steel. The cops looked on benignly as space-age Stockholm got itself temporarily liberated.

Maurice Strong came to the Celebration. He had a good time, too. The folks presented him with their own draft resolution for UNCHE:

TO THE UNITED NATIONS CONFERENCE ON THE HUMAN ENVIRONMENT AND ALL CONCERNED: RESOLUTION NUMBER 86–A, A TEN-YEAR MORATORIUM ON THE KILLING OF HUMAN BEINGS. WE, THE PEOPLE OF THE WORLD who recognize no national or international boundaries, borders, access restrictions, or ownership of our Mother the Earth, do propose that: WHEREAS the United Nations has assumed responsibility for the preservation of species in danger of extinction, and WHEREAS the United Nations Conference on the Human Environment has already adopted a resolution calling for a Ten-Year Moratorium on the Killing of Whales, and WHEREAS the human race is a species so endangered —endangered by political violence, industrial poisoning, social regimentation, territorial competition, apocalyptic weaponry, hunger, greed, etc., and WHEREAS the only way for the human race to survive this century is for us to STOP KILLING each other: BE IT RESOLVED for a trial period of ten years beginning 1 July 1972 all people of the Earth, and all governments purporting to represent these people, be they tribal, local, national or international, recognize Homo Sapiens as an endangered species and joyously proclaim A TEN-YEAR MORATORIUM ON THE HUNTING, KILLING AND ENVIRONMENTAL POISONING OF HUMAN BEINGS.

Strong was moved. "I love your message," he told the happy crowd. "I feel the sense of love in the message. I hope it will get through to all the meetings in which I take part. I hope this message will get through to the whole world."

Strong was also presented with a "Dream Book" in which people had written and illustrated their dreams for the future of the earth. Then the rock band started to play, and people danced and sang and clapped their hands in and out of time to the music and stood around grinning at each other. Some people took all their clothes off.

Sergel's Square was a natural gathering place for all sorts of public happenings. The New Parliament Building,

which housed one-third of UNCHE's meetings, is one of
the shiny high-rises around the square. One floor below the
street, a major station of the subway empties into a large,
open shopping plaza. At street level, housed in the towering
maze of buildings, is the complex heart of the shopping district of downtown Stockholm. Alternative City had a permanent exhibit set up here. The vigil to protest French nuclear
testing at Mururoa Atoll had been held in the open plaza
below the street. The anarchists had demonstrated here the
day before the opening of UNCHE.

One day I was eating lunch at a table by the window of
a restaurant which, being on the second floor of a department store, looked down into the open plaza. To the left
and at street level, I could see the large fountain catching
the sunlight in its spray. A small crowd had gathered to
watch the street theater going on in the lower plaza. Several
of the actors were dressed as trees. Someone fiendish came
by, spraying them with some hideous fantasy chemical. A
rock band accompanied the action, and a man narrated in
Swedish through a microphone, though I couldn't hear him
through the restaurant's plate glass. I saw a girl come trip-
ping by Red-Ridinghood-fashion with her make-believe
lunch in a wicker basket covered with a cloth. As she passed
the trees she began choking and gasping and clutching her
snow-white throat to show that she was overcome by the
noxious vapors. Some action followed which was unintelli-
gible to me, but which I'm sure the narrator made compre-
hensible, and then the scene shifted to a bunch of strap-
hanging Stockholm commuters, wearily making the nightly
trek home, dragging themselves to identical housing units in
the suburbs. The end of another identical day on the corporate treadmill. Each commuter's consolation for this life of
boredom and regimentation, the skit showed, was a refresh-
ing American dose of Coca-Cola, quaffed from a large
cardboard bottle. Thus drugged and fulfilled, the commuters
shuffled off to television and to bed. As I was watching this
pantomime, a pack of a hundred or so cyclists, their faces
covered with white gauze masks against the fumes, rode
through the square, unruffled and holding the honking

traffic behind them down to their own comfortable five or six miles per hour. I guessed it was a demonstration by Alternative City.

The meetings continued too, of course. Another week of "Distinguished Lectures" in the Mirror Ballroom of the posh Grand Hotel, for example. I'd missed most of them, but I made a point of getting myself over there on Tuesday the thirteenth when the Club of Rome's Aurelio Peccei was to speak on human settlements.

I ate lunch in a hurry that day, and got to the Grand Hotel early. It was just as well because I had trouble finding the Mirror Ballroom. As I was wandering about looking lost I ran into Environment Forum's Elisabeth Wettergren, who was just going to sneak another correspondent into the elegant smörgåsbord to which select persons were invited before each of the Distinguished Lectures. As head of the Forum she was such a select person, and she asked me to come along. She whisked us both past a tight-jacketed, gold-braided attendant who was checking invitations, mumbling at him in Swedish that we were both distinguished guests, and we were all in a great hurry to eat so as not to be late for the distinguished lecture, and he wasn't to hold us up with stupid formalities of any kind. The Swedes are impressed by title and rank, and while the attendant stood there with a confused look on his face, we hustled over to the long, beautifully laid table. Again, there were many sorts of herring and salmon, salads, sauces, sliced meats, a variety of cheeses and breads. Since for the second time I'd made the mistake of having eaten already, I restricted myself to tidbits of fish and a piggish-sized piece of strawberry torte with whipped cream. A waitress brought beer to our table. We hurried through our food, then followed the crowd down a hall to the Mirror Ballroom.

The Mirror Ballroom was supposed to resemble Versailles, I guess, dripping with gold filigree flowers and plump *putti*. Mirrors around the walls doubled the extravagance, and rococo chandeliers hung like gaudy crystal cakes from the ceiling. Here in this *salle de bal*, on stomachs laden with delicacies, this very select assemblage was to hear Fiat magnate Peccei delineate the horrors of hunger and over-population.

"Worse than any book of fiction is the prospect of our small planet being invaded by a supplementary batch of three or four billion people in a matter of thirty to forty years," Peccei began after a flattering introduction (on the predictable theme that he needed no introduction) and polite applause. I thought of our small planet as the Mirror Ballroom itself, and that whole "supplementary batch" of invaders squeezing into it. Elisabeth leaned over and whispered something sarcastic in her hoarse, very audible whisper. I chuckled, but the gentleman in front of us turned in his seat and glared. "The next doubling of population by the end of this century or the beginning of the next will have tremendous influence on our collective future and every human problem, including of course that of settling all this swollen mass of humanity." Yes. They certainly couldn't all be invited to the luncheon. Other provisions were going to have to be made.

Peccei made the dubious assertion that "in strictly evolutionary terms, all living creatures have, as their supreme responsibility, that of continuing their own species and making it fitter." However, he based no argument on this teleology, but went on to outline truly horrifying "scenarios for the year 2000 or so of gargantuan megalopolises of thirty, fifty, even eighty million people. The nightmarish vision of these interminable cities is both useful and sobering—for it will prompt people to do everything for it not to materialize. In fact, civilized, wholesome life cannot flourish in these immense conurbations. The possible beneficial effects of any technological fixes [sic] to make them function will be offset by their sheer dimension, the scale factor having a negative value at these levels." Peccei described the Club of Rome-sponsored computer studies done at M.I.T., *The Limits to Growth*, as an effort to understand the human predicament of exponential growth in a finite environment in order for man to be able to continue to shape his own destiny. "Invariably all assumptions . . . point to a single outcome—that if these trends continue the human system will saturate the earth, overshoot its carrying capacity, and finally collapse. This collapse may come in many different ways, but it will invariably endanger not only mankind's standards and quality of life, but also its very possibility of survival. The main conclusion to be drawn from this study is that equilibrium within the human system and between it and its environment will anyhow be reestablished. But it is in our collective interest to plan for it rationally, and not to wait for forces beyond our control to settle it at the cost of tremendous human suffering." The entire complex of problems confronting man, "the macroproblem," he concluded, is comprehended in this question of how "to organize the diverse and separate human settlement on our finite and small planet of the six to seven billion people by the year 2000—and many more in a more distant future. If this macroproblem is not envisioned and its possible solution analyzed now, the danger we all face is that of a gigantic, Darwinian 'battle of the earth' among peoples and nations to secure space, resources, life changes."

Peccei made no attempt to answer the criticism of *The Limits to Growth* made in an earlier Distinguished Lecture by the noted Swedish economist and sociologist Gunnar Myrdal. While admitting that the study "will probably have the useful effect of popularizing the ecologists' broad warnings of the necessity of giving up our expectations of continuing on the road of unrestrained growth," Myrdal had attacked its virtual exclusion of social and political data and concluded that "their system is, therefore, far from inclusive enough to have meaning." Inequities in the distribution of the world's wealth, for instance, are defined in the study as social problems outside the purview of the model. "Particularly in a pretended system analysis," Myrdal said, "it is simply not possible to get away from 'the social problems' merely by stating that they are not taken into account. The ecosystem has to be studied as part of the social system."

As an example, Myrdal cited the distortions in the behavior of the model that result from inclusion of the birth rate as a factor interdependent with the other factors— industrial and agricultural growth, pollution, and the depletion of resources. "The birth rate is . . . quite rightly a factor, and a very important one, within their model. But it is certainly not a function only of the other factors . . . and the interrelations between them all. As we who have studied the demographic development in the several regions of the world know, the movements of these other factors are not even among the most important determinants of the birth rate." Given the study's crude and incomplete data, it was essentially a deception to pretend to simulate a model of world dynamics on a sophisticated computer, Myrdal asserted. The project was characterized by the "quasi-learnedness" that results whenever narrow specialists attempt to study a problem exclusively in, say, economic terms. Moreover, Myrdal's basic criticism, that the Club of Rome's study ignored social problems, seemed to antici-pate not only the ironies of the gilded palace (which adorned Myrdal's speech, too, after all), but also the bizarre perception of those "supplementary batches" of people, in Peccei's speech, as "invaders," as if only certain people were here on the earth by right. One could never quite tell whether Peccei was really well-intentioned, or just phobic about the great unwashed.[1]

During this final week of conference activity there was growing speculation that an impasse had developed in the closed-door committee of the whole to revise UNCHE's declaration. Newspapers began to suggest, cautiously at first, then with ever-greater assurance as the days went by, that the deadlock was hopeless, that the U.N. Conference would issue no declaration at all. Would the whole thing be a bust? people started to wonder. No, UNCHE wouldn't be a bust if there should be no declaration, delegates and officials began telling interviewers defensively. The establishment of the 100-million-dollar environmental fund, of the global Earth Watch monitoring network, of the international data-referral system, of the permanent U.N. Environmental Sec-

[1] Myrdal's address is reprinted in part as "Limits to the Limits to Growth," *The UNESCO Courier* (Jan., 1973), pp. 12–13, and will be published in full by W. W. Norton in a collection of the addresses delivered in the Distinguished Lecture Series.

retariat were all solid accomplishments of which the conference, indeed the world, they argued, could be proud. These
moves to prepare public opinion for an eventual deadlock,
of course, only strengthened the rumors of disaster, and by
balmy Thursday, with only one day of deliberation to go,
deadlock seemed a foregone conclusion.

Personally, I agreed with the apologists; it wouldn't be
a bust if the deadlock resulted in a declaration-less
UNCHE. Nothing could more clearly focus the conflict
between third-world and industrialized nations, and dramatize the staggering problems impeding global cooperation.
After all, the primary reason for UNCHE and its constella-
tion of independent activity in Stockholm was not decision-
making (no resolution of UNCHE is binding on any government), but rhetoric. I mean rhetoric not in a derogatory
sense, but in the true sense as the art of persuasion. Persuasion is what we all went to Stockholm for, and often discord
persuades a good deal better than flat harmony. In any
case, there was an undeniable undercurrent of anticipation
building during the final week as we waited to see if
UNCHE could bring off its declaration.

By the time the committee broke for dinner shortly
after eight o'clock Thursday night, it had come to agreement on twenty-two of the twenty-seven "principles" of the
reworked draft. When the delegates returned from dinner,
UNCHE president Bengtsson joined them at the New Parliament Building for the second time that day to put the
screws on the committee. They were to work through the
night, if necessary, to reach agreement on the declaration
by morning. Indeed, the committee had to work through the
night. By 5:00 A.M. only two of the principles remained in
doubt. One called for the complete destruction of "nuclear
weapons and all other means of mass destruction," to which
China continued to object because chemical and biological
weapons were not specified, and because her own nuclear
weapons, she claimed, were purely defensive and necessary.
The other principle called for states to give full information
of activity within their own borders to neighboring states
whose environments, they had reason to believe, would be

adversely affected by it. Argentina wanted that principle strengthened; Brazil wanted it weakened or deleted altogether. Behind the squabble over "principle" lay the continuing parochial feud between these South American neighbors over Brazil's plans to dam the Paraná River, which flows beyond its borders into Argentina. When the plenary met for its final session the next day, it dealt with these two difficulties by passing the rest of the declaration by acclamation, then passing the principle on nuclear weapons separately over China's objection that the conference should condemn "plunder, aggressive wars, colonialism and neo-colonialism of the superpowers" as the principal causes of global pollution. The principle dealing with publication of information of activity affecting the environment of another country was scrapped, and referred to the coming fall's General Assembly for consideration and debate as a separate measure.

The document that finally emerged from all the drama and political haggling of the revision was remarkably little changed from the original draft. Principles were added calling for protection for wildlife and the oceans. A smattering of Chinese-sounding revolutionary jargon was added to the original formulations. For instance, principle 6 was amended to affirm that "The just struggle of the peoples of all countries against pollution should be supported." And principle 15 admonished that "Projects which are designed for colonialist and racist domination must be abandoned." African countries tacked their special concern incongruously onto principle 1, which affirms the human right to a decent environment, as well as the human responsibility to protect the environment. "In this respect," the principle concludes, "policies promoting or perpetuating *apartheid*, racial segregation, discrimination, colonial and other forms of oppression and foreign domination stand condemned and must be eliminated."

Paragraph 2 of the Preamble added the gratuitous and false piety that "the protection and improvement of the human environment . . . is the urgent desire of the peoples of the whole world."

Paragraph 5 changed the original statement on population, which had stressed merely the problems of over- and under-population, by inserting a more optimistic passage—only slightly revised—from the opening speech of Tang Ke, chairman of the Chinese delegation. "Of all things in the world, people are the most precious. It is the people that propel social progress, create social wealth, develop science and technology and, through their hard work, continuously transform the human environment. Along with social progress and the advance of production, science and technology, the capability of man to improve the environment increases with each passing day." The fact that the conference could adopt words taken from the same speech that the U.S. had condemned as "inappropriately laden with political and ideological invective," showed the strength of China's leadership of third-world countries at Stockholm. It was most significantly the injection of "third-world perspective" that distinguished the final declaration from the draft, not least in the attitude evident in this last quoted statement on population. People, the third world was saying, are not primarily a problem, but a resource.

"In the developing countries most of the environmental problems are caused by underdevelopment," the revised Preamble declared. "Millions continue to live far below the minimum levels required for a decent human existence, health and sanitation. Therefore, the developing countries must direct their efforts to development." What "development" in this context means seems assumed, although in actual fact it is far from clear. The drafters apparently have in mind more of what has already polluted the West.

Principle 7 of the draft had stated that "environmental deficiencies generated by the conditions of underdevelopment pose grave problems and can best be remedied by and in the course of development," to which the revising committee added "through the transfer of substantial quantities of financial and technological assistance as a supplement to the domestic effort of the developing countries and such timely assistance as may be required." This hard-nosed attitude toward the costs of environmental protection, which

many third-world people see as a luxury that only the affluent nations can afford to pay, determined the most significant additions to the draft. It is one thing for the
industrialized nations to endorse the need for development
consistent with environmental protection. It is quite another
for them to bear a fair and responsible share of the costs.
Underdeveloped countries can ill afford to divert the meager
resources they possess from capital investment to pollution
control. This realism lies behind the next principle in the
revised document: "For the developing countries, stability
of prices and adequate earnings for primary commodities
and raw material are essential to environmental management since economic factors as well as ecological processes
must be taken into account." This means that industrial
nations ought not to take advantage of the vagaries of the
market to obtain at the lowest possible price the raw materials on whose sale underdeveloped nations depend. In
effect, the policy demands global price supports as a form of
aid from the affluent to the deprived.

Development requires not only capital, but technology,
and technology in turn requires a continuing flow of scientific information. Here too, the underdeveloped nations are
at an obvious disadvantage, since they have neither the
expertise nor the educational or research facilities to promote the most advanced science and technology. Thus, the
committee added to the original principle—"scientific research and development in the context of environmental
problems, both national and multi-national, must be promoted"—the specification "in all countries, especially the
developing countries. In this connexion, the free flow of
up-to-date scientific information and transfer of experience
must be supported and assisted, to facilitate the solution of
environmental problems; environmental technologies should
be made available to developing countries on terms which
would encourage their wide dissemination without constitut-
ing an economic burden on the developing countries."

But even the revised United Nations Declaration on the
Human Environment stopped short of seeking the roots of
the environmental crisis in the prevailing social, political,

and economic systems. It did not question the fundamental worth of the present modes of technology in industrial nations. It tacitly accepted the basic values that govern the uses to which that technology is put. It said there are serious problems in the world that have global dimensions that need tending to, but it was not a revolutionary statement.

The mood at the final UNCHE plenary was buoyant and self-congratulatory. Everyone but the Chinese was delighted with Shirley Temple's hopeful speech. The Chinese did not smile and they did not clap, but sat among the applauding delegates as though nothing were happening around them. There were other speeches, with profuse thanking on behalf of everyone of the host country and city, and much expressing of gratitude for the skillful leadership of conference president Bengtsson and conference secretary-general Strong.

Strong also made a speech, in which he praised the work of the conference, of course, but also warned against overconfidence. "Mr. President, we have earned the right to a moment of self-congratulation at the close of this historic Conference. But we must not allow this mood to delude us about the ability of established Governments and international agencies to bring about the changes that must take place or to carry through on our decisions without the active participation of many groups outside the official structures of governance." In particular he praised the concern evidenced by the work of nongovernmental groups in Stockholm. "An unprecedented degree of public interest in our preparations and now in our present deliberation has been demonstrated by the presence here of nearly 1500 representatives of the mass media and more than 700 accredited observers from non-governmental organizations. These voluntary, professional and scientific organizations along with press, radio and television have all served to alert governments and inform the public about present and future environmental perils and in so doing they have focused the world spotlight on our work. Non-governmental organizations in particular have stimulated a two way exchange of ideas and information that have made major contributions to the success of our deliberations. I now look forward to their initiatives and co-operation in the future environmental work of the UN."

This cooperative venture between official and non-official bodies, Strong went on, has revealed how the necessary global decisions must be made in the future. "We must now actively seek to broaden the base of decision-making in environmental affairs. We must add a new dimension to the discourse between governments and peoples, engaging the best technological and managerial abilities of the entire world. The global environment has a global constituency. The community of the concerned is now no less than the world community." To judge from Strong's speech anyway, the independent activity in Stockholm had had a profound effect. "Mr. President, I believe that, as we leave now, we must do so with determination to build on the foundations we have laid here in Stockholm. If we do not, then this Conference will have been a brief flash, a meteor burning its way through the blackness of space." The plenary stood and applauded Strong unflaggingly for several minutes to show their genuine admiration for the man who had steered this conference through such tricky waters. The Chinese, it's true, applauded only very delicately, joining their palms repeatedly without adding appreciably to the noise that filled the hall. But others were unrestrained. At last Strong humbly put his own palms together, and bowed to the delegates in a sign of peace. UNCHE was over.

Later that day at Dai Dong's closing program in the ABF House, Dean Abrahamson, professor of public affairs at the University of Minnesota, took up the question of the relationship of the general public to official institutions in the matter of environmental protection. The new U.N. environmental agency will, he said, be a bureaucracy like all other governmental organs. Like any bureaucracy, left to its own devices it will develop systemic inertia and a self-justifying, self-fulfilling mode of operation which will keep it from serving its real public function. We can expect it to respond only to continual public pressure. The contemporary difficulty in maintaining public vigilance over government, however, is caused by the increasingly technical nature of the problems, and thus of the information required to deal with them. An informed public, then, will depend on independent scientists willing to speak to them uncondescendingly and to provide them with the information they need to come to sound conclusions of their own, rather than merely to represent the interests of industry and government or "disinterestedly" pursue their own research. Scientists, in other words, must accept a responsibility to the public, a responsibility that in the past they have often shrugged off or scorned.

Margaret Mead had agreed to join the final Dai Dong panel to represent the "NGO" statement, which she had apparently had a major hand in writing, and which she had read aloud to the plenary of UNCHE. The NGOs (observers from Non-Governmental Organizations, representing groups as diverse as the Sierra Club, International Planned Parenthood Federation, Congress of African People, World Wildlife Fund, Socialist International, European Oceanic Association, International Chamber of Commerce, International Alliance of Women, and United World Federalists, to name only a few) had formed themselves into a loose affiliation, with the purpose of functioning as a U.N. booster organization, liason between the official U.N. structure and independent groups of citizens eager to advance its aims and programs. Their statement paralleled UNCHE's own declaration, for the most part, and pledged continuing support for the U.N.'s work. "We reaffirm the concept of organized citizen support for the work of the United Nations. . . . We therefore intend to urge our organizations to mobilize and expand their membership in support of the work of the United Nations in general and the Environmental Secretariat in particular."

Asked from the audience about the stumbling block to global cooperation—national sovereignty—Margaret Mead replied that we should concentrate positively, on the development of "planetary loyalty," rather than negatively, on attacking the concept of sovereignty. *Planetary loyalty* put me suddenly in mind of a person I'd met during the first

days of the Dai Dong Conference. The evening of the party
for the Indians I had been hurrying down the dirt road from
Graninge in a rush to catch the five o'clock bus to town.
With me was a man who had been videotaping the Dai
Dong Conference. His pinched features and broad face
were like the moon's. It was a warm evening, the sun still
over the horizon, and he was sweating in his dusty leather
trench coat. His shoulders sagged under the weight of two
large leather bags in which he carried his equipment. They
hung down on thick straps, almost to his knees. Stringy hair
grazed his shoulders, and he had a sparse, yellowish goatee.
We chatted and puffed as we walked, occasionally breaking
into a dog-trot past the scattered summer houses and gardens. In one of the gardens a man was trimming stalks of
rhubarb.

The videotaper asked me, as though it really mattered,
where I was from. As it happened, I explained, I was
about to move from just outside Philadelphia to just outside New York. We walked on.

"Where are you from?" I asked after a pause.

He looked straight ahead, not breaking his stride, holding the bags to his sides to keep them from swinging violently. "From the planet, man," he said finally. There was
more than a hint of condescension in his tone. To be from
the planet was apparently a state of mind you hadn't
attained if you still thought you were just from Philly. I
didn't ask which planet. What was he videotaping for? I
asked. Astral projection, probably, I thought.

He explained that he was an itinerant alternative news
service, carrying hip planetary news to alternative communities around the U.S., mostly New Mexico, he said. He
went around recording the *real* news to show to folks who
wanted to know what was *really* happening. "Where am I
from?" he repeated. "What does that mean, man? I'm not
from anywhere. I'm from, like, everywhere. The planet, man.
The planet."

Margaret probably had something different in mind,
something less exclusive than total cosmic illumination.

Replying to a young Rhodesian on the panel who was representing OI Committee International and who had spoken against all the mere conferences and counterconferences, all the mere talk, all the mere writing of papers and declarations and books, and had called for action instead of talk, she attacked the political divisiveness among (and even within) the various groups at Stockholm, all of whom should have been working together for the common cause of environmental protection and social justice. She likened the politics that governed the aims and tactics of the OI group ironically to the politics within the United Nations itself. Both organizations, she said, were hamstrung by it. Millions of women and babies throughout the third world would have to suffer because population growth had become a political "football," and the concept of population control political taboo.

The Rhodesian had attacked such positions on industrial growth as those of the NGOs, the *Ecologist*'s "Blueprint for Survival," and *The Limits to Growth*. To blame growth per se, he had said, is to hide the real political source of environmental deterioration, namely the profit-motivated system of production. Margaret Mead rejected this argument. The NGO position need not be defended against the attacks of the OI Committee, she said. The NGOs are concerned with environment; OI is concerned with revolution. She concluded by noting the irony that all the concepts, the ideas, the jargon in terms of which third-world revolutionaries speak are purely Western inventions, including "freedom," "liberation," even the concept of "the third world" itself. She had come to Stockholm, she said, to talk about *people*, not politics.

"To talk about people *is* to talk about politics," the Rhodesian answered.

Gonzalo Fernos, Puerto Rican architect and participant in the Dai Dong Conference, also an accredited NGO observer to UNCHE, stood up in the audience and denounced the NGO statement as utterly devoid of third-world perspective. He also attacked Margaret Mead's role in writing the document, accusing her of being merely a "self-appointed spokesman" of the NGOs and of misrepresenting the real range of opinion among them.

Margaret grabbed the microphone in front of her, glared at Fernos, and said that she had come here on Dai Dong's invitation to talk about the NGO statement, not to be insulted. Furthermore, she was not "self-appointed," but had been *asked* by others to help prepare the statement, *asked* to read the statement in the plenary, *asked* to take part in this panel discussion, and so on. And so forth. And things sputtered on for a few minutes more as the battle-weary audience began drifting out of the auditorium at the end of a long three weeks. We were all a bit cranky. It was time to go home.

I went upstairs to the Dai Dong office where I'd parked my bags—the suitcase, the briefcase, the trombone, and the bright orange duffel bag I'd had to buy to carry the thirty-odd pounds of papers and tapes home. Even though it was warm, I had to wear my corduroy jacket with the big pockets to stuff more things into. Juggling those four heavy bags, one under each arm and one in each hand, first onto the bus, then off again, down into the subway, putting the bags down each time to reach for my wallet to show my pass, picking them up again, then through the long underground passageway to the train station, I was sweating and seedy, and I felt abused as a coolie, and the thought that this was perhaps a rare chance at third-world perspective wasn't a consolation. A cold beer was a consolation, though, and that was the first thing I got myself when I finally could put down my bags in the waiting room. I was meeting the friends with whom I'd stayed after the Dai Dong Conference ended; we were taking the same midnight train south —Loffe and Annika and their two girls.

When the train was ready for boarding we found an empty compartment and hoped we could have it to ourselves. We closed the door inhospitably and spread the five of us as wide as we could over the two facing benches, but after a while two American girls with knapsacks came in and sat down. They sure hoped this was the train to Copenhagen, they said wearily. It was, I told them, but this particular car terminated in Malmö. They'd have to go a few cars further back for Cophenhagen. They sighed, picked up their knapsacks again, and walked through to the back of the car. We grinned at each other, stretched out again and waited for the train to pull out.

At midnight, we heard the outside doors of the cars slamming shut up and down the length of the train. We put the window down and leaned out to watch the people waving good-by on the platform moving past us, slowly at first, then faster and faster, as though not we, but only the platform was moving, like a conveyor belt. As the end of the platform passed, the train shot suddenly forward into the dark open space of the city. Stockholm's towers and spires performed a stately quadrille, rows of street lights and the moving lights of cars weaving pearl-string patterns around them. We stayed at the open window of the train silently watching until the last glimmer of the city had disappeared. Then we closed the window except a crack for air, and set to work on the bread and salami and the dozen cans of beer Loffe had packed along for our midnight supper. The beer lasted us far into the night and made it easy to sleep stretched out on the two seats and floor in between. Loffe saved one can for his breakfast.

Appendix:

An Independent Declaration on the Environment

Human beings live as a part of a complex natural system with aspects of interdependence which have only recently become dramatically evident. They are also a part of complex social, economic and political systems which they themselves have created, usually without an appreciation of the unpredictable and sometimes disastrous effects of such systems on the life-giving capabilities of nature. These systems, moreover, contain faults and imbalances which prevent them from responding equally to the needs of all people, but provide a minority with a surfeit of goods, while leaving the greater part of the world's people in poverty and despair.

The interaction between the social and natural systems on this planet has in our time resulted in an environmental crisis which, although it can be traced largely to the economic practices of the industrial nations, effects every person on earth. The awareness of the environmental crisis has come at a time when the deprived nations and the poor and deprived people in all nations are struggling for power to control their own destinies and asserting their right to full participation in national and world affairs. The survival of humanity demands that the condition of the natural environment and the needs of human beings be considered as interrelated parts of the same problem. This will require profound changes in our political, economic and social structures on the one hand and our individual life-styles on the other, with the aim not only one of survival, but of survival with the maximum possibility of human fulfillment. It will also require massive programs of education to enable people to understand the interrelatedness of the world's problems, and the kinds of changes that need to be made. In such endeavors, certain guiding principles must be followed.

I. *Human survival depends upon the life activities of uncounted thousands of species of plants, animals and microorganisms, and upon intricate physical and chemical reactions in the atmosphere, oceans, fresh water, and on the land.* The vastness and complexity of this interdependence have recently become evident with increasing human intervention into the life-giving processes of our planet. All life is dependent on the interactions of matter and energy carried out in earth's ecosystems. It is these interactions which we are altering, even before we fully comprehend them. The people of the world must come to understand them, to preserve them and, when altering them, to do it with care and wisdom.

II. *There is a fundamental conflict between traditional concepts of economic growth and the preservation of the environment.* During the last century, uncontrolled continuous growth in the industrial production of environmentally harmful substances and products in some regions of the world has produced dangerous amounts of pollution and has been responsible for an inordinate waste of resources. At the same time, an increasing concentration of economic power and industrial activity has led to a centralization within a few nations of the benefits from the use of the earth's natural resources, and the international political influence that is derived from the control of these resources. It has become clear that a more rational distribution of industrial power is necessary if the global problems of environment and society are to be solved. Such a redistribution would achieve at the same time a more equal apportionment of economic and political benefits among nations and individuals.

III. *The exploitation of Third World national and regional resources by foreign corporations, with a consequent out-*

flow of profits from the exploited regions, has resulted in a vast and growing economic disparity among nations and a monoply of industrialized countries over production, energy, technology, information and political power. Complementary to this is the flooding of developing countries with surplus goods and capital, with a resultant distortion of their economies, and the deformation of their environments into monocultures in the interest of further enriching the industrial states. The foreign investments, economic development and technological practices of such industrial states must be curbed and altered by the basic claim of a region's people to control of its resources. Use of these resources, however, should not be dictated by the accidents of geography, but must be allocated in such ways as to serve the needs of the world's people in this and future generations. The authority of any region's people over resources and environment must include the obligation to recognize that the environment is an indivisible whole, not subject to political barriers. The environment must be protected from avoidable pollution, destruction and exploitation from all sources.

IV. *It is obvious that human population growth cannot continue indefinitely in a finite environment with finite resources. At the same time, population is one of a number of factors, no one of which in the long run is the most important or the most decisive in affecting the human environment.* In fact, the question of population is intrinsically inseparable from the question of access to resources. A true improvement in the living conditions of the people of developing countries would go further in stabilizing population growth than programs of population control. Population is not a single problem, but one which has a complex interrelationship with the social, economic and natural environments of human beings. Population size may be too small or too large at any particular time depending on the availability of natural resources and the stresses on the environment. The ecological principle regarding the role of population is equally applicable to human and animal populations. However, in human populations social organization is such as to change or modify this principle.

On a global scale, the population problems of the developing countries have coincided with the colonial expansions of the last two centuries, and the exclusion of Third World populations from full access to their own resources. This process of economic exploitation still continues in spite of the nominal independence of various former colonies and dependencies. Meanwhile the alliance between economic elites in the developing countries and industrial interests in the metropolitan countries makes it impossible for the people of the Third World to use their resources to fulfill their own needs. The redistribution of resource use on a global level is an unconditional prerequisite for correcting this historic process.

As long as resources are wasted, as they manifestly are, it is deceptive to describe population growth as if this were the source of all evils. There is obviously a confusion in many people's minds between overcrowding and population, but the fact that some urban areas grow like cancers should not serve as a pretext to divert attention from the real task of our generation, which is to achieve proper management of resources and space. Those nations that are mainly responsible for this state of affairs have certainly no right to recommend population-stabilizing policies to the world's hungry peoples.

It should be noted that, for economically developed countries, the combination of an increase in industrial consumption per capita with a stable population, or of stable consumption per capita with a growing population, will both lead to further resource depletion and pollution. This need not be true if the appropriate socio-economic changes that will lead to an ecologically sound production and consumption pattern are made.

V. *Economic development of any kind will require technology*. Much conventional technology and many of its proliferating products have proved ecologically harmful. We cannot reject technology *per se* but must restructure and reorient it. Ecologically sound technologies will minimize stresses to the environment. A rapid development of the new approach should be complemented by a technology review and surveillance system to assure that any new technology is ecologically compatible and will be used for human survival and fulfillment. It is not enough to add anti-pollution devices to existing technologies, although this might well be the initial stage of phasing out present polluting technologies.

VI. *The culture of the industrial nations reflects their political and economic ideology, and is based on an ever-increasing accumulation of material goods and an uncritical reliance on technology to solve humanity's problems.* This ideology, in which the ethical element is a forgotten dimension, is spreading throughout the world; its acceptance will not only cause individual and national disappointment and frustration, but will make rational economic and environmental policies impossible to carry out. An increase in economic well-being will help deprived countries preserve their own cultural and spiritual heritages, but many people in industrial countries, faced with a reduction in their material possessions, will need to find new definitions of progress in values compatible with environmental and social well-being.

VII. *Among the most critical problems that constitute an existing and accelerating threat to human survival is war.* Even apart from the colossal cost in human suffering that all forms of war entail, arms expenditures place an overwhelming economic burden on rich and poor nations alike, and an equally heavy burden on the environment. Military technology, being such a large part of industrial activity, particularly in economically developed countries, is a major cause of global pollution and resource depletion. Thus, war and preparation for war are both directly related to environmental problems. With nuclear proliferation, both civil and military, the environmental hazard has become increasingly critical, arms control more difficult, and nuclear war more probable. The enormous sums consumed in military expenditures must be applied directly to the task of global redistribution and environmental improvement. As long as we tolerate the waste and the destructiveness of war itself, we cannot achieve the stable environment on which the survival of all of us depends.

Yet the determination to abolish war must be accompanied by a recognition of the right of peoples to struggle, and the certainty that they will struggle, to liberate themselves from national and international systems that oppress them. Those who most earnestly seek an end to war must affirm their solidarity with their fellow humans engaged in such a struggle, while simultaneously insisting on the need to develop effective nonviolent methods of solving the social and international conflicts of a world in danger of an annihilating war.

Participants in the Conference and Signers of the Declaration

Samir Amin, Senegal. Director, Institut Africain de Développement Economique et de Planification, Dakar.

Mohamed Zaki Barakat, Egypt. Faculty of Medicine, Azhar University, Cairo.

Heinrich Carstens, Germany. Chairman, Friends World Committee for Consultation.

Donald Alfred Chant, Canada.[2,3] Chairman, Department of Zoology, University of Toronto.

Mohammed Ahsen Chaudhri, Pakistan. Head, Department of International Relations, University of Karachi.

Dora Obi Chizba, Nigeria. President, African Environmental Association.

Jerzy Chodan, Poland. Head Department, Agricultural College, Olsztyn.

Purushottam Jaikrishna Deoras, India.[2] Professor, Haffkine Institute, Bombay.

Peter Dohrn, Italy. Secretary, Mediterranean Association Marine Biology-Oceanology.

Yusuf Ali Eraj, Kenya. Former President, Family Planning Association.

M. Taghi Farvar, Iran.[1] Center for the Biology of Natural Systems, Washington University, St. Louis.

André Faussurier, France. Director, Centre de Reflexion et d'Etudes Scientifiques sur l'Environnement, Lyon.

Gonzalo Fernos, Puerto Rico. Chairman, Environmental Quality Commission, College of Engineers, Architects and Surveyors.

Nicholas Georgescu-Roegen, U.S.A.[2,3] Distinguished Professor of Economics, Vanderbilt University, Nashville.

Thich Nhat Hanh, Vietnam (in exile). Buddist monk, poet, educator.

Bengt Hubendick, Sweden.[2] Director, Naturhistoriska Museet, Göteborg.

Jaime Hurtubia, Chile.[1] Professor, Institute de Ecologia, Universidad Austral de Chile.

Conrad Alan Istock, U.S.A. Professor, Department of Biology, University of Rochester.

Fred Harold Knelman, Canada.[2] Professor, Humanities of Science Department, Sir George Williams University, Montreal.

Satish Kumar, India. Writer. Founder of London School of Nonviolence.

Jean Mussard, Switzerland. Former Director, United Nations Conference on the Human Environment, presently Managing Editor, *Revue Polytechnique*.

Cao Ngoc Phuong, Vietnam (in exile). Professor of Biology, Universities of Saigon and Hue.

Jurgenne H. Primavera, Philippines.[1] Professor of Biology, Mindanao State University.

Henry A. Regier, Canada.[2,3] Professor of Zoology, University of Toronto.

---

[1] M. Taghi Farvar, Jürgen Schütt-Mogro, Jurgenne Primavera, and Jaime Hurtubia have signed the Declaration subject to the following rewording of the first sentence of Point IV:

Population is not the most important or the most decisive factor affecting the human environment, although it is apparent that human population growth cannot continue indefinitely in a finite environment with finite resources.

[2] Nicholas Georgescu-Roegen, P. J. Deoras, Bengt Hubendick, Donald A. Chant, Henry Regier, and Fred Knelman have signed the Declaration subject to the following footnote to Point IV:

In several parts of this document, the environmental issues have become largely submerged in statements more relevant in one of a number of ideological polarities. A current controversy, concerning the quantitative measure of significance to be attached at this point in time to the various aspects of "population factor" in comparison

Henryk Sandner, Poland. Professor of Biology, Polish Academy of Sciences.

Jürgen Schütt-Mogro, Bolivia (in exile).[1] Former Professor, University of La Paz.

Rudi Supek, Yugoslavia. Professor of Sociology, University of Zagreb.

Jun Ui, Japan. Lecturer, Department of Urban Engineering, Faculty of Engineering, Tokyo.

Roel Van Duyn, Holland. Author. Leader of Kabouter Party.

Arthur H. Westing, U.S.A. Professor of Botany, Windham College, Vermont.

Ernst F. Winter, Austria. Director of Transnational Research Center, Katzelsdorf.

Signed June 6, 1972

Chairman of Conference: Hannes de Graaf, Utrecht, Holland.

Director of Dai Dong: Alfred Hassler, Nyack, New York.

Deputy Director of Dai Dong for Europe: Jens Brøndum, Copenhagen, Denmark.

---

to other important factors, has confused the issue. The differences provoking the scientific controversy in themselves do not concern directly the point we make here: In various places and at various times the "population issue" has become or will become critical, being preceded or followed in time by other critical factors not closely related to the population factor.

[3] Nicholas Georgescu-Roegen, Donald A. Chant, and Henry Regier have signed subject to the following rewording of the final paragraph of Point VII:

Those who most earnestly seek an end to war call upon the nations who are oppressing or may in the future oppress militarily, economically, or politically other nations or sectors of their own populations to desist from such actions. They also call upon those who are now or will in the future be the object of oppression to refrain from violence and to act so as to expose the aggressor and deny him the possibility of invoking the pretext of self-defense and, thus, of continuing or triggering new wars.